Decision Analysis
An Integrated Approach

Decision Analysis
An Integrated Approach

Andrew Lang Golub
John Jay College of Criminal Justice

John Wiley & Sons, Inc.
New York • Chichester • Brisbane • Toronto • Singapore • Weinheim

Acquisitions Editor	Beth Lang Golub
Assistant Marketing Manager	Leslie Hines
Illustration Coordinator	Anna Melhorn
Senior Production Manager	Linda Muriello
Production Editor	Melanie Henick
Manufacturing Manager	Dorothy Sinclair

This book was composed in Times New Roman using WordPerfect by Henrietta Golub and printed and bound by Braun-Brumfield. The cover was printed by Lehigh Press.

Library of Congress Cataloging-in-Publication Data

Golub, Andrew Lang.
    Decision Analysis : an integrated approach / Andrew Lang Golub.
        p.   cm.
    Includes bibliographical references.
    ISBN 0-471-15511-X (paper)
    1. Decision-making. I. Title.
HD30.23.G64   1997
658.4'03 - - DC20   96-35433
                                                                          CIP

Printed in the United States of America

10 9 8 7 6 5 4 3 2 1

CONTENTS

PREFACE

This book provides the basis for the comprehensive study of procedures for making good decisions. It is intended for use in a one-semester course for upper-level undergraduate or professional Master's degree students. The material can be covered in a more intense half-semester course for Master's degree students with prior exposure to economics, accounting, and probability. The book is also designed to serve as the methods book to supplement a set of case studies for a Master's degree course in decision analysis or policy analysis.

The material covered in this book is nearly self-contained. However, a prior course in either probability or statistics is useful. Appendix C provides a review of the principles of probability used in this book. Students with additional prior coursework in probability, statistics, economics, organization theory, and psychology will develop even richer insights from the study of decision analysis.

The chapter organization follows the ten steps of the rational model for decision making: (0) Develop agenda, (1) Define the problem, (2) Identify objectives, (3) Identify alternatives, (4) Forecast outcomes, (5) Compare outcomes, (6) Select an alternative, (7) Implement the decision, (8) Monitor the implementation, and (9) Evaluate the result. Chapter Zero corresponds to step 0, developing the agenda. Chapter Zero also provides an overview of the rational approach and discusses the criticisms of insensitive rationalism. Chapters One through Six correspond to steps 1 through 6 and comprise the decision analysis phase. The last three steps are more administrative in character. These steps are discussed, briefly, in Chapter Zero. A comprehensive discussion of these three activities is beyond the scope of this book.

The book provides extensive information on problem definition, too much for a single chapter. As a result, this material has been divided into three smaller chapters. Chapter One-A describes the basic activities involved in defining a problem. Chapter One-B presents additional technical details regarding the representation of a problem as either an influence diagram or a decision tree. Chapter One-C presents how to solve a decision problem. Technically, in terms of the rational model, Chapter One-C belongs at the beginning of Chapter Five on comparing alternatives. Indeed, Chapter One-C was isolated from the rest of the material on problem definition to allow instructors to conveniently postpone coverage of this material. On the other hand, it can be beneficial to teach students the techniques for representing and solving decision problems, simultaneously. Additionally, learning the solution technique at the beginning of the semester can help foreshadow the progression of ideas for the rest of the semester.

The book provides supplementary material in a series of appendices. Appendix C reviews the basic probability concepts necessary for use of this text and is designed for potential inclusion before Chapter Four. Appendix D discusses the time-value of money and can be optionally included before Chapter Five, if time permits.

The text is designed to help students with a term project of solving their own decision problems from start, selecting a problem, to finish, preparing a recommendation. Such personal involvement provides a practical reason for reading about and trying each of the techniques described in this text. Each chapter starts by identifying its central objectives and ends with a summary, exercises, suggestions for applying the concepts to the course project, and references for further reading.

The use of DPL, a decision support program, is highly recommended. This analyst-friendly program provides a bookkeeping service for collecting insights into a problem as they occur and can be used throughout the course for working on a project. DPL also calculates a recommended course of action based on all the information specified. Ultimately, DPL provides succinct graphics for presenting a conceptualization of a problem and a justification for the recommendation. Appendix A provides a short guide to use of DPL for the types of analysis presented in this book. It is intended for potential inclusion before Chapter One-B. It contains a tutorial suitable for use in a computer classroom or for self-study.

Less detailed analyses can be accomplished with hand calculations or use of a spreadsheet. Appendix B provides a short guide to use of spreadsheets for decision analysis.

I would like to thank the folks at Applied Decision Analysis who produce DPL for creating such an excellent product. This product has made the application of many decision analysis techniques available to a wide range of people in a straightforward manner. From the moment I saw it, I was inspired by the elegant simplicity of its user interface. I was also greatly inspired by Robert Clemen's book, *Making Hard Decisions*, which epitomizes the interdisciplinary and practical aspects of decision analysis. *Decision Analysis: An Integrated Approach* was written in this tradition: to draw together the knowledge and techniques that are useful for making decisions without prejudice to the discipline in which it was developed, and to present these techniques in a manner that makes them accessible to the widest possible audience.

In preparing this book, I received much professional assistance. I would like to thank the staff of John Wiley & Sons for their role in helping to coordinate the various aspects of this project from obtaining reviews through marketing the book. In particular, I would like to thank Joe Heider, Amy Hegarty, Leslie Hines, Anna Melhorn, Shelley Flannery, and Maddy Lesure. I would like to extend a special note of appreciation to Bonnie Lieberman and Will Pesce for their support of the project.

I would also like to thank my reviewers for their insightful comments: J. Etezadi Amoli of Concordia University; Adam Borrison of Applied Decision Analysis; Ben Bowling of Cambridge University; Anna Goldoff of John Jay College; Don Keefer of Arizona State University; Karen D. Loch of Georgia State University; James E. Smith of Duke University; Adina Schwartz of John Jay College; Refik Soyer of George Washington University; and Rakesh Vohra of Ohio State University. Additionally, I would like to thank all of the students who have taken my courses on quantitative decision for their questions that have helped me to refine my presentation of decision analysis concepts.

I am greatly indebted to my mom, Henrietta Golub, for an outstanding job composing the layout of the book. I would also like to thank my dad, Fred Golub, for reviewing the manuscript. Most of all I'd like to thank my wife, Beth Lang Golub, for her encouragement, for her helpful comments, for publishing this book, and for all the good times. I consider her, and our two kids, Abby and Milo, my best decisions, ever.

ABOUT THE AUTHOR

Andrew Lang Golub is an assistant professor of Public Administration at John Jay College of Criminal Justice, City University of New York. He is also a member of the Doctoral Faculty of City University of New York and a principal research associate at National Development and Research Institutes, Inc. He received a Bachelor's and a Master's degree in operations research and industrial engineering from Cornell University in 1981 and 1982, respectively. He received his doctorate in public policy analysis from the Heinz School of Public Policy and Management of Carnegie Mellon University in 1992.

Dr. Golub's current research examines social problems with an aim toward helping develop more effective and efficient government programs. His recent publications have examined drug abuse, the spread of HIV/AIDS, and the life course of individuals who engage in criminal behavior. Previously, he has worked as an analyst for AT&T, Eastman Kodak, Exxon, and the U.S. Department of Transportation.

Chapter Zero
THE CONTEXT OF DECISION MAKING

OBJECTIVES
After studying this chapter you should be able to

- concisely identify why any particular decision is hard to make,
- describe the ten steps of the rational model for decision making,
- discuss the difficulties inherent in applying the rational model.

Making decisions is an important part of everyone's professional and personal life. In this sense, we are all *decision makers* and can all benefit from studying techniques for decision making. *Decision analysis* is the interdisciplinary field which examines how to improve decision making. Decision analysis is also the process of studying any specific decision. Some problems are so complicated and so important that the individuals who analyze the problem are not the same as the individuals who are responsible for making the final decision. Therefore, this book distinguishes between a *decision analyst*, someone who studies what decision to make, and a decision maker, someone responsible for making the decision.

This book presents a step-by-step procedure for decision making known as the *rational model*. The various steps incorporate techniques from economics, cognitive psychology, and probability. The book describes how to perform each step, in detail, and illustrates their application in a variety of situations. These

1

applications are based on real problems. However, most of them describe hypothetical concerns of fictional decision makers.

The rational model can be used to solve a wide range of problems. On the other hand, this approach does have its limitations and has been criticized for a variety of reasons. A skillful decision analyst needs to determine when to use this approach, how to supplement rational analysis, and when to use only parts of the approach. This chapter introduces the context for decision making by describing the need for good decision-making skills, introducing the steps of the rational model, and examining the criticisms of this model.

MAKING GOOD DECISIONS

A good decision is the end result of carefully selecting a preferred course of action after studying what might happen were a variety of alternatives chosen. The emphasis in this definition is placed on the process of making the decision and not on the decision itself.

Sometimes it is not easy to tell whether a decision was good simply by examining the course of action chosen. This is true because of two factors: the risk involved in the decision, and the decision maker's personal values. Regarding risk, the future cannot always be predicted accurately. So decision making involves the assessment and possible acceptance of risk, based on the information available at the time of the decision. Sometimes, even when a good decision is made, things turn out badly, purely because of chance. Regarding preference, a good decision should fully reflect the decision maker's values. Two decision makers presented with similar choices could make different selections because of their differing tastes. In this case, each decision would have been a good decision. Thus, to determine whether an individual made a good decision it is more important to examine the process that led to the selection of an alternative than to examine the alternative selected.

The rational approach to decision making can be used to solve personal, business, and government problems. The following paragraphs list various decisions commonly faced in each domain. The context of decision making differs across domains with respect to the substantive knowledge necessary to support a good decision and the constituency who has to be satisfied by the decision. The basic principles for making a good decision are the same in each domain.

Personal Domain. People commonly ask themselves and others questions such as the following: Where should I live? What college should I go to? Which career should I pursue? Which medical treatment should I follow? How should I invest my money? Which car should I buy? Which computer system should I buy? which microwave oven? which coffee? There are a variety of self-help publications that offer relevant advice, including *What Color Is Your Parachute, Places Rated Almanac*, and *Consumer Reports*. These publications provide data and suggest techniques to help people make informed decisions.

Business Domain. Companies routinely ask themselves operating questions such as the following: Should we relocate corporate headquarters? Where should we build our newest franchise? Who should be president of the new division? Which computer system should we buy?

Businesses also ask important long-term or strategic questions like the following: How should we position our company for the future? Which research areas should we pursue? These decisions are more similar to the policy problems faced by government organizations, listed below, than to the operating decisions listed above.

Government Domain. Government organizations regularly ask questions such as the following: Should we institute a universal health care program? How should we cope with social problems such as crime, unemployment, rampant violence, and drug abuse? To what extent should we intervene in conflicts abroad such as in Cuba? Bosnia-Herzegovinia? Iran? Somalia? The ongoing analysis of such problems is typically referred to as *policy analysis*.

Government organizations also ask many important short-term questions regarding day-to-day operations, such as the following: Who should be appointed director of the agency? Where should the new fire station be located? Should we run our own garbage hauling program or contract the service to a private concern? Which computer system should we buy? These problems are more similar to the operating decisions faced in the business domain than to the policy concerns listed above.

Why Decisions Are Often Hard to Make

Making a decision can be hard for a variety of structural, emotional, and organizational reasons. The structural reasons include uncertainty, a tradeoff among competing concerns, and overall complexity. For many decisions, if we could predict the future we would know just what to do, but we can't and so we don't. Such problems often involve either accepting a risk or not. This book presents techniques for incorporating uncertainty directly into the decision-making process using subjective probability and risk preference.

Uncertainty: Milo's Homemade Ice Cream, Part I

Milo is thinking of opening a home-made ice cream store. This investment represents a major commitment on his part. Purchasing all the equipment would require most of his savings and preparing the store would require six months of hard work. If the store is successful, he would be financially secure for the rest of his life. However, if the business failed he would lose a lot of money. If he knew that the store would be successful, then he would definitely go for it. But he doesn't know.

Many decisions are made difficult by the existence of a tradeoff. Sometimes choosing an alternative that best meets one objective necessitates sacrificing on another objective. This book presents formal techniques for making such tradeoffs known as *multiattribute utility theory*. Sometimes no alternative seems acceptable. In such situations, a new alternative that no one has previously thought of may be necessary. This book presents creativity-enhancing techniques that can be used to help find such solutions.

Multiple Objectives: The North American Free Trade Agreement

In 1993, the United States was faced with the question of whether to ratify the North American Free Trade Agreement, which would reduce tariffs on goods traded between the United States, Canada, and Mexico. On the face of it, the United States should obviously sign the agreement since reduced tariffs would promote the international exchange of goods and services, and thereby improve everyone's quality of life.

However, public sector problems are intertwined and the resolution of one problem typically leads to the creation of others. By reducing tariffs, Ross Perot (and others) warned that reducing tariffs would cause many companies to move their manufacturing operations from the United States to Mexico, which has lower wages and less environmental regulation. In this regard, tariffs help protect American industries, maintain workers' rights, and protect the environment.

Thus, the decision ultimately revolves around a tradeoff between promoting international trade or protecting domestic industries. Ultimately, the United States chose to sign the North American Free Trade Agreement.

Some decisions are hard because there are too many considerations involved. This book presents influence diagrams for systematically developing a convenient representation of a complicated problem. Using these diagrams, a decision analyst can systematically develop a picture that identifies the various elements involved in a decision and their interrelationships. Subsequently, the analyst can concentrate on specifying the important details associated with each element. Once the problem has been fully specified, a computer can be used to perform the complicated calculation associated with determining the most advantageous course of action taking into account all the details of the problem.

Complexity: Snapple

In 1994, Phil Marineau, President and Chief Operating Officer of Quaker Oats, faced the decision whether to acquire Snapple, producers of popular all-natural soft drinks. Snapple's appeal sprung forth in the early 1990s fed by concerns about chemical additives, nutrition, and natural foods and a New Age sensitivity.

Its spreading popularity took some of the fizz out of the soda industry long dominated by Coca Cola and Pepsi Cola.

Because of its widespread sales, the purchase of Snapple would be very expensive. However, as a large food conglomerate, Quaker Oats could potentially increase sales by capitalizing on their well-established marketing and distribution channels. Hence, Snapple appeared to be a very desirable acquisition.

Furthermore, Quaker Oats could streamline the operation of Snapple by subsuming much of the function of middle and upper management within Quaker Oats, as the parent corporation. Layoffs of redundant and expensive executives would further increase profitability. On the other hand, this homogenization of management could stifle any further creativity associated with the Snapple product line, and greatly reduce the value of the purchase.

Another line of reasoning suggested that this New Age movement is a passing fad and the free-flowing demand for Snapple would dry up in time. In this vein, Quaker Oats could postpone any purchase for five years, as a test of the product line's enduring appeal. However, in the interim another company could acquire Snapple, the purchase price could go up, or Quaker Oats' financial condition could worsen.

Has anyone's head started to swim?

There are two other factors that can make decision making hard that are not discussed in subsequent chapters: anxiety and consensus. These concepts can be best understood through the study of organizational theory. Anxiety results from the heavy burden of being a decision maker (or recommending a decision) and therefore accepting responsibility for what happens. As an individual, you must live with your choices. In a business, when things go wrong the individual responsible may get fired. In government, when times are tough the incumbents are often ousted through the electoral process. Hence, making good decisions is crucial to one's future in any domain.

Anxiety: Hypermedia, Part I

The information revolution is continuing to bring us new ways to store and examine information. For example, entire encyclopedias are now available on CD-ROM and consume much less shelf space than their hard-copy predecessors. Most importantly, programs that retrieve information now use hypermedia techniques that allow the user to conveniently access information nonsequentially. For example, the main screen for ADAM, a hypermedia anatomy program, is a picture of a human body. To learn more about a specific body part, the user can select it with a mouse, zoom in to observe greater detail, and click on various icons to obtain further information about its function. This interactive experience provides a user-friendly alternative to the standard anatomy book where one manually searches indexes, turns pages, and reads line-by-line and word-by-word to obtain the desired information.

ABC Publishing is considering opening up a new division to develop and sell hypermedia products. This could be a brilliant plan, assuring industry leadership well into the next century. On the other hand, starting a new division with a high-tech product would be very expensive. If the product were not widely successful within a few years, the division could cause considerable financial strain to the company.

Should ABC Publishing open a hypermedia division? What if ABC Publishing opened a hypermedia division and it was not successful? Would you then say that they had made a bad decision? How about if they do not open a hypermedia division, and hypermedia comes to dominate the information market and in the process marginalizes the role and profits of traditional book publishing companies? Would you then say that ABC had made a bad decision?

Anxiety results from not always being able to predict the future with accuracy, and yet having to make a decision. Decision analysts distinguish between a good decision and an *unfortunate outcome*. A decision must be made ex ante, before any uncertain events occur. Hence, a decision should be evaluated based on what was known at the time the decision was made and how well that information was used. On the other hand, final outcomes are evaluated ex post, after all uncertain events have occurred. Even when a good decision is made, chance events can lead to an unfortunate outcome and regret over opportunities missed, the "I should have bought IBM stock in the 1960s" syndrome. Consequently, even good decision makers are subject to emotional anxiety and regret.

Here are some suggestions to protect yourself as a decision maker:

- Get the best possible information you can given the constraints of time, money, and personnel in order to make the most informed decision.

- Prepare a document detailing the basis for your decision, so there will be no question of the ex ante basis for your decision.

- Socialize your information and recommendation with a wide variety of people to verify the reasonableness of your analysis.

- Whenever possible, incorporate the opportunity to revise your decision at a future date after uncertain events have prevailed. In the hypermedia example, ABC Publishing could postpone forming a hypermedia division, determine what indicators would suggest a burgeoning new market, and plan to enact the division as soon as possible, once those conditions prevail. This would provide a low-cost safety valve for reversing their decision if and when the situation changes.

In many decision-making contexts, a consensus must be reached before a decision is implemented. Organizational structures and cultures are quite varied and present an additional challenge to the decision analyst. The most general advice for working within an organization is to present a comprehensive analysis and be certain that it reflects due consideration of the concerns of everyone involved.

Why a Course on Decision Analysis?

Many of the concepts presented in this book will appear quite obvious and reflect things you already knew, figured out on your own, or learned within the study of another discipline. This should be reassuring. Other techniques might be new to you. The primary purpose of this book is to put all of these ideas together, along with the software available to support their application, as a step-by-step procedure for making important decisions when you have time to perform analyses. The insights developed from learning these techniques should also help improve your judgment and your ability to make decisions informally and quickly.

People have been making decisions since the origins of human intelligence. The ability to choose is the nature of free will, as opposed to instinct. Similarly, people have been trying to codify how to make good decisions for a very long time. In 1772, Benjamin Franklin–an interdisciplinary scholar, philosopher, scientist, entrepreneur, patriot, and diplomat– responded to a query from his friend Joseph Priestley as to whether to accept a job offer. His advice was as follows[1]:

> I cannot, for want of sufficient premises, advise you what to determine, but if you please I will tell you how. . . . My way is to divide half a sheet of paper by a line into two columns; writing over the one Pro, and over the other Con. Then during three or four days' consideration, I put down under the different heads short hints of the different motives, that at different times occur to me for or against the measure. When I have thus got them all together in one view, I endeavor to estimate the respective weights. . . . [to] find at length where the balance lies. . . . And though the weight of reasons cannot be taken with the precision of algebraic quantities, yet when each is thus considered, separately and comparatively, and the whole matter lies before me, I think I can judge better, and am less liable to make a rash step; and in fact I have found great advantage for this kind of equation, in what may be called moral or prudential algebra.

---

[1]Paraphrased by Robyn M. Dawes in *Rational Choice in an Uncertain World* (1988) Orlando, Harcourt Brace, p. 202, from Bigelow, J., ed. (1887) *The Complete Works of Benjamin Franklin*, New York, Putnam, p. 522.

This procedure strongly resembles multi-attribute utility theory presented in Chapter Five.

In the second half of the twentieth century, our knowledge about how to make decisions has been enriched by advances from numerous contemporary disciplines, especially economics, cognitive psychology, probability, and computer science. Additionally, many decision analysis principles have been developed and taught in other interdisciplinary contexts, including policy analysis (typically taught in political science), strategic planning and management science (typically taught in business administration), operations research (typically taught in engineering), and systems analysis (typically taught in computer information systems).

THE RATIONAL APPROACH TO DECISION MAKING

The rational model provides a comprehensive and systematic ten-step approach to decision making. Each step indicates an essential activity and builds upon the preceding steps. For example, an analyst is better prepared to identify objectives after developing a clear statement of the problem. Hence, it is natural to go through the steps in order. On the other hand, analysts typically revisit steps as an understanding of the problem grows. Continuing the previous example, an analyst might revisit the problem definition step due to insights into the nature of the problem clarified while identifying the objectives.

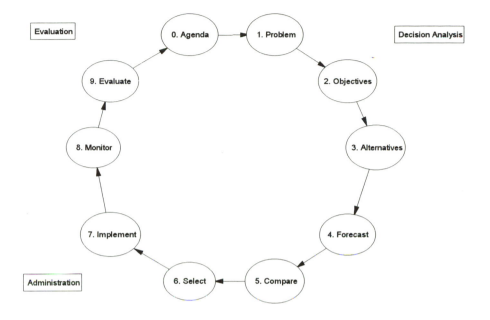

The Ten Steps of the Rational Model

The chapters in this book are arranged according to the analytic steps of the rational model, from problem definition through selection of an alternative. The administrative steps of the rational model—agenda setting, implementation, monitoring, and evaluation—are discussed briefly in this chapter. The ultimate success of a decision may depend on anticipating careful implementation. As an important reminder of the connection between analysis and administration, implementation, monitoring, and evaluation are included as central steps in the rational model for decision making. Notwithstanding, a careful and appropriately detailed discussion of the importance of these steps in each of the three decision-making domains is beyond the scope of this book.

Set Agenda. Prior to performing any decision analyses, someone needs to determine what problems will be studied, a practice known as *agenda setting*. Many government decision-making organizations formally publish their agenda on an ongoing basis. For example, the Supreme Court of the United States prepares a docket of cases to be studied each session. The U.S. House of Representatives goes one step further. The House Rules Committee not only determines which problems will be on the agenda and in what order, they also allocate a limited amount of time for the discussion of each item. In general, the place on the agenda and amount of time allotted to a problem reflect its relative importance and sense of urgency.

Define Problem. The first step to addressing a problem is to clearly identify it. As an operational guideline, a problem can be defined as the difference between a current and some preferred situation. Once clearly defined, the problem can be studied further to identify its scope, its relationship to other problems, its causes, and its impact. A comprehensive understanding of the problem can help guide further analysis toward its resolution.

Identify Objectives. Once a problem has been clearly identified, the next step of the rational approach to decision making is to identify the underlying reason(s) for addressing the problem, called the *objective(s)*. One such reason, called the *primary objective* is contained in the operational definition of the problem. It is the reason why the decision analyst values the preferred situation to the current situation. Other objectives can include additional reasons for addressing a problem and side effects that could result from addressing the problem. Solving most problems in the personal, business, and government domains involves spending money. Clearly, the less money spent the better. So, saving money is typically included as an objective in most decision analyses and as the only important objective in some. Identifying objectives helps to clarify the purpose of the analysis and provides a framework for comparing the various alternatives.

Identify Alternatives. The search for a solution to the problem starts by identifying a group of reasonable responses to the problem, called *alternatives*. Because the final choice must be selected from the alternatives considered, it is important that the "best" solution be included in the analysis. However, the best solution is typically not known in advance. More often, there are several alternatives that seem plausible but imperfect. Furthermore, the analyst's understanding of what is the best solution may change with further study of the problem. There is no universal technique to guarantee that a list of alternatives includes the best solution. Comprehensiveness, however, can act as a substitute. The more complete the set of alternatives considered, the more likely the best alternative is included.

Forecast. The choice among alternatives must be guided by a vision of what the future would be like were each implemented. This vision is known as a *forecast*. There are a variety of ways to express one's understanding of a situation ranging from a variety of mathematical models to written scenarios describing how things tend to operate. Quite often, a forecaster will identify his or her uncertainty by suggesting that one or possibly another future could result from implementing a specific alternative. These various postulated futures are called possible *outcomes*.

Compare. At this point, the analyst has enough information to compare the forecast for each alternative, according to the objective(s) of the problem. A table such as the one presented below, which summarizes how each alternative fares according to each objective, is called a *scorecard*.

	Alternative 1		Alternative 2		. . .	Alternative J
Final Outcome	1A	1B	2A	2B		
Probability	P_1	$(1 - P_1)$	P_2	$(1 - P_2)$		
Objective 1						
Objective 2						
. . .						
Objective I						

Select. If any one alternative scores the highest on all objectives, this option is said to *dominate* the others. In this case, that alternative is the obvious best choice. However, quite frequently one solution is the best on one objective and another alternative is best according to a different objective. To resolve such tradeoffs, the decision analyst must identify the relative importance of each objective. Based on a weighting system reflecting these values, the analyst can determine which forecasted outcome has a "best" combined value across all objectives and select an alternative course of action.

Moreover, selection is the transition between the decision analysis and administrative phase of the rational model. At this point, the analyst double-checks the basis for the recommendation and contemplates how to present the results to the decision maker(s).

Implement. Once an alternative has been selected, subsequent success depends on how well the plan of action is executed. Implementation can be viewed as a process of converting a variety of inputs into the solution of a problem, as illustrated in the diagram below. The *inputs* to the process should include a plan, appropriate authorizations, and the essential resources of sufficient money, appropriate personnel, facilities, and equipment. The physical activity required to execute the course of action is referred to as the *process*. The direct result of this process is referred to as the *output*. The effect or satisfaction obtained from the output is referred to as the *impact*.

The Implementation Process

Implementation: The Broad Street Bridge

Traffic congestion in downtown Springfield has become intolerable, particularly during rush hour. The town has decided to replace the old two-lane bridge into town with a new four-lane span. In order to implement the decision, the town council must authorize the construction and allocate sufficient funds. These are essential inputs to implementing the alternative. The city manager has been placed in charge of hiring a construction firm and monitoring their progress. The process phase of the implementation involves building the bridge. The final output will be a four-lane bridge. It is hoped that the impact of this increased capacity will be an end to rush-hour traffic congestion.

Monitor. An alternative may fail to achieve its desired effect for three possible reasons: (1) Theoretical Failure: The idea was faulty in the first place; (2) Chance Failure: Chance events frustrated the alternative's effect; (3) Implementation Failure: The alternative was not properly executed. Monitoring is the oversight employed to insure that a decision has the greatest possible chance of achieving its desired effect by making sure it is correctly implemented. This includes checking the process at each point in the conversion process. Were adequate resources allocated? Were reasonable procedures followed? Were sufficient outputs created? Did it have the desired impact?

Evaluate. Evaluation serves to identify the extent to which the original problem was resolved. Such analysis can identify whether and how much additional corrective action might be appropriate.

The final arrow in the rational model depicted on page 8 indicates that if a problem is sufficiently unresolved it should be placed on the agenda again and a new analysis undertaken. This is particularly important to bear in mind because many problems tend to persist in spite of corrective action. In the public sector, issues such as unemployment, foreign relations, and crime must be constantly addressed. Similarly, businesses must constantly focus on developing products and services with a comparative advantage in the face of changing global markets, while containing operating costs and maintaining corporate morale. For such constant concerns, application of the rational model can result in a spiral, wherein analysis repeatedly passes through the sequence of steps and the result is continual long-term improvement.

CRITICISMS OF THE RATIONAL APPROACH

The structured approach of the rational model has been broadly criticized as being unrealistic in a variety of ways. These arguments typically fall into three categories: (1) the overwhelming difficulty of comprehensive analysis, (2) the apolitical emphasis on "the problem" and not on the people involved, and (3) its dependence on human reasoning which is inherently flawed. These criticisms suggest the larger context in which decisions are made. A skillful analyst will consider when and how to supplement the rational calculations used in identifying a preferred solution to a problem.

Difficulty

It must be emphasized that the application of the rational model can be time consuming. The following case study looks at two attempts to create a rational procedure for developing the budget for the U.S. Government. It appears that the amount of time spent on budget analysis ended up restricting the amount of time that individuals had to do their jobs.

> **Difficulty of Comprehensive Rational Analysis: U.S. Budget Reform**
> In 1965, in an attempt to control government spending, Lyndon Johnson established the Program Planning and Budgeting System [PPBS] (Johnson, 1992, pp. 414-416). This rational procedure required each agency to define its major objectives, state how they would be obtained, and justify its expenditures.
> Similarly, in 1977, Jimmy Carter instituted Zero-Based Budgeting [ZBB]. The central principle of ZBB was that no program should be automatically entitled to any funding; rather, the initial federal budget starts at $0. Each subsequent dollar appropriated to a program must be justified as worthwhile.
> Both PPBS and ZBB sound fiscally responsible. Why should any program that is not worthwhile receive funding? However, the reality of implementing both PPBS and ZBB at the federal level proved to be exceedingly cumbersome. The amount of work in continually providing detailed justifications for programs (whether worthwhile or not) resulted in a profusion of paperwork and overtime, but little reduction in expenditures. Perfection may not be an attainable or even a worthwhile goal when it comes to federal budgeting.[2]

Evidence suggests that many decision makers tend to follow a rational procedure, but that they reduce the difficulty of the analysis by cutting corners. Herbert Simon analyzed how executives actually make decisions. He found that they tended not to even try to develop a comprehensive list of all possible alternatives; rather, they selected a handful of reasonable ideas for consideration. Moreover, they did not search for the "best" overall alternative; instead, they

---

[2]Rationalism is not the exclusive province of either Democrats or Republicans. PPBS and ZBB were both established by Democratic Presidents. More recently, it has been the Republicans who have advocated for increased rationality. In 1981, Ronald Reagan instituted Executive Order 12291, which mandated that no regulation may be enacted unless the potential benefits to society outweigh the potential costs. In response, Democrats complained that this procedural constraint would block or delay imposition of rules to protect the environment and worker safety.

selected one of the first candidates that satisfied the minimum requirements on most objectives, a procedure Simon termed *satisficing*. For his work on the application of what is known as *bounded rationality*, Herbert Simon received the Nobel Prize for Economics in 1978.

The key lesson here for decision analysts is that not all problems warrant a comprehensive analysis. The most comprehensive analyses should be reserved for especially important problems. Thus, the role of agenda setting is paramount. In general, a busy decision analyst should establish a reasonable amount of time for the study of each problem and tailor the analysis to meet the deadlines as close as possible. Given time constraints, not all analyses can be totally comprehensive. In some cases, offhand approaches such as satisficing may be appropriate. However, for important decisions when more time is available, a good analyst should be able to do better.

Lack of Political Sensitivity

Rational analysis has been criticized for focusing too much on the problem and not enough on the difficulty of implementing a decision. Such criticisms have been loudly voiced in the domain of governmental decision making where the importance of consensus building is paramount. The lack of political sensibility seems less relevant to business and much less relevant to personal decision making, because the power to make and implement decisions is often concentrated in only one or a few key individuals. However, the lack of political sensitivity often associated with rational analysis can also help explain the resistance to change that can occur in the business and personal domains. In general, people who are not involved in making the decision may become resentful and resist its implementation.

During the 1960s and 1970s, many government analysts tended to ignore political issues and optimistically recommended radical change (Heineman et al., 1990, pp. 16-17). Moreover, these analysts claimed that in setting government policy we should put aside our own parochial values and select the "objectively best" solution to any problem. The process of setting aside one's values is known as maintaining *value-neutrality*. The unbridled enthusiasm for value-neutrality and lack of humility on the part of these government analysts led many people who were less technologically optimistic to resent their efforts.

Today, it is more widely recognized that there is no objectively best standard to use for solving every problem. Most importantly, any recommendation for solving a problem is inherently based on some set of values. As a result, many analysts will present the values they used in any analysis and then present why these values are reasonable and fair.

Cost Benefit Analysis The primary technique for supposed "value-neutral" decision making is *cost-benefit analysis* [CBA]. The central principle of CBA is to choose the most efficient or "best" alternative as measured by the ratio of its expected benefits to its cost (benefits/costs). This objective favors those alternatives that provide substantial benefits and those that have relatively low costs. A variation of this procedure is *cost-effectiveness analysis*. This technique uses a criterion for selecting the "best" solution that is slightly different from that of CBA. In cost-effectiveness analysis, the analyst selects the alternative that provides the largest net benefit calculated by subtracting the costs of the alternative from its benefits (benefits - costs).

Both cost-benefit analysis and cost-effectiveness analysis require that the analyst convert all costs and benefits into a common currency before the arithmetic can proceed. Hence, a large literature has developed around the question of putting a dollar value on *nonmonetary quantities* not typically sold in any store (such as time spent commuting and level of pollution), and *intangible qualities* (such as the good name of a company, employee morale, and scenic parkland), which are even harder to place a price on.

An extensive branch of this literature deals with precisely how much of a premium should be placed on safety. The essential tradeoff on safety issues is the cost of increased prevention weighed against expected fatalities. To answer such questions in the cost-benefit framework requires a specific dollar value be placed on a human life.[3] CBA suggests that once these dollar values are assigned then an objective "best" alternative can be selected. However, the price of a human life is a very subjective quantity and answers will differ widely across individuals.

Cost-Benefit Analysis: Inflatable Air Bags for Automobiles
Airbags are safety devices located in a car's dashboard which rapidly inflate when a car is involved in a major impact. These pillows provide greater restraint than traditional seat and shoulder belts and can save a person's life in a major accident. However, they are expensive and can add as much as $1,000 to the price of a car.

Should the U.S. government require that all cars provide air bags in order to reduce traffic fatalities? The federal government makes decisions like this regularly. Whether a safety feature becomes a requirement depends on the number of lives that the feature can be expected to save as opposed to the cost of implementing the feature, a classic cost-benefit analysis. In this case, the cost of requiring manufacturers to include air bags on all new cars was deemed to be too much, compared to the number of lives that would be saved. However, many manufacturers decided to include air bags as standard equipment anyway, because they knew that their customers were safety conscious.

---

[3]Peter Passel (1995, January 29), How much for a life? Try $3 to $5 million, *New York Times*, p. 3, provides an informed overview of the research and decision-making controversy surrounding issues of human safety.

The central focus of CBA, a comparison between costs and benefits can provide an excellent organizing structure for careful decision making. However, this procedure is not value neutral. The price an individual places on any nonmonetary objective is inherently subjective. For example, incorporating a decision analyst's subjective price for a human life destroys the value-neutrality of a cost-benefit analysis. Some would argue that it is immoral to place a price on a human life. Advocates of CBA, however, argue that by deciding whether to implement a safety feature, the decision maker is implictly setting a price on human life. In using CBA, the analyst is just making that cost explicit.

Incrementalism   In practice (especially during the 1970s), cost-benefit analysts have often mistakenly excluded or undervalued those nonmonetary quantities and intangible qualities that are hard to convert into dollars. One particular value is the cooperation and morale that can develop when workers know that they are respected members of a productive organization. Rational analysis has often been used to justify sweeping organizational changes that disrupt individual routines. Noting this problem, critics of the rational approach suggest that change at any time be limited to minor deviations from the current situation. This approach to decision making is known as *incrementalism*.

There are several important reasons for advocating incrementalism. These reasons can be divided into organizational and political issues and are well illustrated by the following example of the attempt by United States to implement national health care during the early 1990s.

Incrementalism: National Health Care

In 1992, Bill Clinton was elected to the presidency of the United States partly on the strength of his promise to provide a simplified program for universal access to health care. Upon election, he appointed one of his most trusted advisors, Hillary Rodham Clinton, to head a committee of experts in designing a comprehensive system.

Understanding the structure of the present health-care system presented a major challenge to the committee. Which institution is in charge of health-care delivery in the United States? Clearly, the Department of Health and Human Services has some oversight responsibility, although their control is quite limited. In actuality, health-care delivery depends on a complex web of interactions among a variety of autonomous organizations including hospitals, insurance companies, pharmaceutical companies, doctors, nurses, other medical professionals, and lawyers. This system evolved through the cooperation and coordination of these and other parties responding to the myriad issues involved in health-care delivery.

Even before the Clinton proposal was revealed, lobbyists for insurance companies, pharmaceutical companies, and doctors argued that any changes would lead to declines in service quality and dramatic increases in costs. In the end, the proposal was defeated.

Decision making can be thought of as an abstract geometry problem. All the possible alternatives to a problem and their variations can be thought of as points in a diagram, such as the one presented below. The range of all possible alternatives is called the *decision space*. In the diagram, x indicates the current situation. A comprehensive analysis might determine that the most desirable situation is quite different from the current situation. The location of this "best" solution is indicated with an asterisk (*) some distance from the current situation. Based on the diagram, the rational analyst would recommend implementing the "best" alternative. Why settle for anything less?

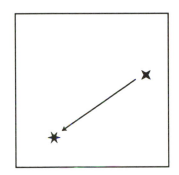

x current situation
* best situation
Decision Space and the Rational Model

Incrementalists would strenuously object to such a recommendation and call it incredibly naive. These analysts would argue that * may be preferred to x but the path from one to the other is fraught with dangers. There are many reasons why such a radical change can cause problems. These reasons are summarized as three alternative models for understanding how change can occur: the organizational, disorganizational, and political models.

Organizational Model The *organizational model* starts with the realization that programs, particularly in the government domain, are implemented by large institutions that coordinate the activities of many individuals. These organizations tend to evolve a protocol for handling different types of interactions called *standard operating procedures*. Changes to these procedures typically require changes throughout an organization, are expensive, and will not work smoothly for some time. Hence, any proposed change should be consistent with current procedures, perhaps allowing for slight modifications. This limited range of potentially acceptable changes to the current situation is illustrated in the following figure.

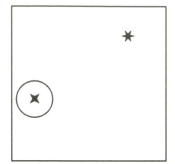

x current situation
* best situation
– limit of currently feasible alternatives

Decision Space and the Organizational Model

Any radical change requires unlearning the current procedures for doing things and learning new ones. Such an activity is extremely expensive and disruptive to the lives of individuals already working within the system. From an organizational perspective, only those solutions that draw upon an institution's standard operating procedures should be considered. These alternatives comprise the limited range of alternatives depicted around the current situation in the diagram above.

Disorganizational Model. Another organizational perspective emphasizes the fact that a policy is often not the result of a coherent agenda of a single agency, but the end result of various actions by different agencies tossed together. This perspective has been called the *garbage can model* (Johnson, 1992). However, the name *disorganizational model* of decision making seems quite appropriate because it contrasts this perspective with the strong, orderly vision of the organizational model's emphasis on standard operating procedures.

Abstractly, this perspective suggests that an alternative should not be depicted as a single point in a universe, but, rather, as a collection of points each representing a different agency's role. A current situation represents the sum total of all of these activities. The figure below shows that a policy change could involve the simultaneous shifting of procedures in all of these organizations. Proponents of the disorganizational model advocate that change should come slowly and incrementally, given that the change to any one agency could have unexpected and undesirable consequences.

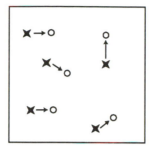

x current situation
○ best situation

Decision Space and the Disorganizational Model

Political Model The *political model* suggests that decision making is not centralized. Therefore, it is not possible for one individual to implement a comprehensive solution. Moreover, there really is no single best policy. There are many different best policies, each of which is best for a different individual or group of individuals. The parties who are interested in any given problem are called *stakeholders*.

The following figure depicts this model as a collection of alternatives most preferred by each stakeholder. Given the various groups jockeying for their interests, any chosen policy represents a compromise among the various best policies. Those groups with more power tend to draw the current policy closer to their interests. A policy change occurs when the influence of one or more groups changes leading to a new compromise solution.

x the current compromise situation
* situation most desired by some constituency

Decision Space and the Political Model

These incremental models suggest that use of the rational model, especially in the governmental domain, be tempered by additional sensitivities. The decision analyst should be aware that radical change results in a large organizational cost. This expense should be seriously considered and weighed against the benefits of any major programmatic changes. Regarding political considerations, the conscientious analyst should include the concerns of all stakeholders affected by a decision in an analysis.

Sensitive application of the rational model can incorporate the concerns raised by the organizational and political perspectives. Most importantly, it is not enough for an analyst to identify the "best" solution. To insure that a policy gets implemented, a decision analyst should support administrators charged with implementing decisions by preparing a detailed implementation plan that is sensitive to organizational and political concerns. Better yet, involving the stakeholders and individuals in charge of implementation in the decision-making process could possibly increase the likelihood that the chosen course of actions will be accepted and executed smoothly.

Limitations of Human Reasoning

The foundation of rational decision making is the ability of human beings to look objectively at a problem and use logic to deduce the "best" course of action. Much recent literature, particularly in philosophy, suggests that humans are not able to look at a situations objectively. More fundamentally, this literature suggests that there are no absolute truths and that what an individual accepts as knowledge is a product of how a culture prepares the individual to view a situation. This view is sometimes called *postmodernism*. This perspective has a long tradition both in Western and Eastern culture. Many of the issues pondered by postmodernism are reminiscent of Zen Buddhism.

Limitations of Objectivity: The Westward Expansion of the United States

During the nineteenth century, the United States expanded from its original thirteen states along the eastern coast of North America to the western coast bounded by the Pacific Ocean. Prior to the 1960s, most history books used in American grade schools discussed the expansion of the United States into a great nation in terms of the challenge presented by bloodthirsty attacks by savage Indians who roamed the land.

Books written more recently often take a more sympathetic view of Indians, who are now known as Native Americans. They had been called Indians because Christopher Columbus had thought he had found a shortcut to India when he landed on North America. The new name is intended to correct this mistake. It is now taught that these Native Americans had a rich cultural heritage and that at numerous times they were treated poorly by the European interlopers.

Which view is correct: savage Indians or righteous Native Americans? Postmodern scholars suggest that both views are wrong. Writers of history approach their job with their own particular mindsets and look for facts to support their perspectives. No matter how hard a scholar may try to be objective, life experience colors his or her perspective. Postmodern scholars go on to argue that objective truth does not exist and that all knowledge is *socially constructed*, defined by an individual's overall view of the world.

Furthermore, an individual's place in a culture will color his or her perspective. Postmodern scholars use this theory to argue that what people think they see varies across race and gender. Postmodern activists argue further that the voice of women and ethnic minorities must be heard to balance the overly dominant white male perspective.

In addition to questioning the existence of objectivity, postmodern scholars question the usefulness of logic. Logic is inherently flawed. Therefore, any conclusion reached by logical deduction might be affected by such flaws, particularly if it is based on a biased view of the world. Postmodern scholars conclude that an overdependence on logic can be dangerous.

Limitations of Logic: A Card Trick

Here is an experiment that illustrates a limitation of logical deduction. A primary foundation of logic is that any statement can be evaluated as either true or false. However, this foundation is shaky. There are actually statements that are neither true nor false. They are *unknowable*.

Take a blank index card or a sheet of paper. Write on one side, "A: The statement on the other side is true." Turn the card over and write, "B: The statement on the other side is false."

Is statement A true? Try to evaluate this proposition logically. Assume that statement A is true. This statement says that the statement on the other side, statement B, is also true. So, if statement A is true then statement B is also true. Next, evaluate whether statement B is true. This statement says that the statement on the other side, statement A, is false. However, this represents a logical contradiction since it was assumed that statement A is true. On this basis, it can be concluded that statement A is not true.

Is statement A false? Try to evaluate this proposition logically. Assume that statement A is false. This statement says that the statement on the other side, statement B, is true. So, if statement A is false then statement B must also be false, too. Next, evaluate whether statement B is false. This statement says that the statement on the other side, statement A, is false, which is what was assumed. Therefore, statement B is true. However, this represents a logical contradiction since it was assumed that statement A is false, which implied that statement B is false. On this basis, it can be concluded that statement A is not false.

This analysis indicates that statement A is not true and not false. Logically then, statement A is unknowable. (This concept of unknowability can be confusing.)

Postmodern scholarship suggests that analysts not become overly dependent on their calculations. An enlightened decision analyst is aware that his or her understanding of a problem is colored by life experiences. Therefore, to get a richer appreciation of a problem it is important to listen to the voices of others, particularly those whose life experiences are different.

❏ SUMMARY

Decision analysis provides techniques and insights to improve decision making in the personal, business, and government domains. Decisions can be hard because of uncertainty about the future, the necessity to make tradeoffs among competing objectives, and the overall complexity of a problem. Decision analysis provides methods for dealing with each of these problems. Decision making can also be hard because of anxiety with having to live with a decision and because of difficulties in reaching a consensus when final decision-making authority is spread among individuals.

The rational approach prescribes a series of ten steps for comprehensive decision analysis and implementation: (0) Agenda Setting, (1) Problem Definition, (2) Objective Identification, (3) Alternative Identification, (4) Forecasting, (5) Comparing, (6) Selection of an Alternative, (7) Implementation, (8) Monitoring, and (9) Evaluation. These steps form a cycle, particularly since many problems need to be revisited regularly. Agenda setting is the process of determining which problems should receive formal analysis and how much time should be allotted to each. The problem definition stage entails identifying how the current situation differs from some preferred situation. This activity leads into the identification of objectives for resolving the problem.

Once the analyst has an adequate understanding of the problem context, he or she can proceed to identifying reasonable alternatives for consideration, forecasting what would happen were each implemented, comparing these outcomes according to the stated objectives, and finally selecting the most appropriate alternative. Subsequently, administrators are charged with implementing the decision, monitoring its progress, and evaluating the results of the chosen alternative. In the business and governmental domains, different individuals or agencies are often charged with decision analysis, decision making, implementation, monitoring, and evaluation. In the personal domain, you may perform all of these roles.

Use of the rational model should be tempered by an understanding of the administrative context in which decision making occurs and of the limits of human reasoning. The effort involved in formal analysis can be immense. Hence, not all problems merit a comprehensive analysis. The analyst should be aware of reasonable time constraints imposed. Additionally, the conscientious analyst should take into account the organizational difficulty involved in making large changes and the interests of all stakeholders affected by a decision, especially in the governmental domain.

❒ EXERCISES

1. Identify ten decisions in each domain (personal, business, and government).

2. Janet, a 72-year-old retired executive in generally good health, underwent a treadmill test at her physician's office recently. The doctor diagnosed her as having a silent ischemia, suggesting that she had major blockage of the arteries bringing blood to her heart. The danger of a silent ischemia is that the patient does not even suspect a heart problem since other body systems tend to compensate for the deficiency. However, Janet was told that if she let it go untreated she had a substantial risk of suffering a heart attack in the next few years, which could kill her. Unfortunately, bypass surgery was determined to be the treatment for her condition. Bypass surgery involves substantial pain, and there is always the possibility of not surviving the treatment or side effects. Should she have the surgery?

    a. Why is this decision hard?
    b. What choice must be made? What uncertainties complicate the decision? Why is this decision important?

3. Choose a decision from each domain in Exercise 1 that appears to be hard and answer the following:

    a. Who is responsible for making the decision? Why is the decision hard?
    b. What choice must be made? What uncertainties complicate the decision? Why is this decision important?

4.   Identify a decision that seems to be best understood from the perspective of the organizational model.   Discuss the organization's range of standard operating procedures, and what types of simple changes might be considered.

5.   Identify a decision that seems to be best understood from the perspective of the disorganizational model.   Further identify the role of the various institutions responsible for administering some portion of any solution.

6.   Identify a decision that seems to be best understood from the perspective of the political model. Further identify the primary objective of each constituency affected by the problem's resolution.

7.   Identify how each step of the implementation process will be realized for each of the following solutions.   Indicate what inputs are needed, the process of implementing the alternative, the outputs of the process, and the intended impact.   Describe how the process could be monitored at each point.

     a.   Reduce the spread of AIDS through a needle exchange program.
     b.   Start a new division to produce men's hats.
     c.   Block the building of a convenience store in the neighborhood through a community effort.

☐ FOR YOUR PROJECT

1.   Choose a problem for your extended term project for this course.   This topic may be one of the problems identified in Exercise 1 or a new topic.   However, your problem should relate to an area in which you are already knowledgeable.   Making good decisions involves having good information and using appropriate techniques.   This course emphasizes the use of techniques, and it would be best if you did not need to acquire much more information.

2.   Prepare a short memo identifying the problem you plan to study throughout this course.   Briefly describe the problem and the nature of your association with it. Discuss why this decision seems hard and why the decision is important enough to merit extended formal analysis.

3.   Identify the problem: Identify the characteristics of your ideal situation and how the current situation differs from it.

4.   Organizational issues: Describe the current situation and identify any institutional arrangements that are in place that tend to support the status quo.

5.   Political issues: Identify each person or group who cares about your decision (stakeholders).   Identify the key concerns and apparently favored solution of each stakeholder.

FOR ADDITIONAL INFORMATION ON

Models of decision making:

Allison, Graham T. 1971. *Essence of Decision: Explaining the Cuban Missile Crisis*. Boston: Little, Brown.

Dunn, William N. 1994. *Public Policy Analysis: An Introduction*, 2nd ed. Englewood Cliffs, NJ: Prentice Hall.

Johnson, William C. 1992. *Public Administration: Policy, Politics, and Practice*. Guilford, CT: Dushkin Publishing Group.

Incremental models of decision making:

Kelly, Marisa and Steven Maynard-Moody. 1993. Policy analysis in the post-positivist era: Engaging stakeholders in evaluating the economic development districts program. *Public Administration Review*, 53(2):135-142.

Lindblom, Charles E. 1959. The science of muddling through. *Public Administration Review*, 19:79-88.

White, Louise G. 1994. Policy analysis as discourse. *Journal of Policy Analysis and Management*, 13(3):506-525.

The organizational context of decision making in business:

March, James G. and Herbert A. Simon. 1958. *Organizations*. New York: Wiley.

Schermerhorn Jr., John R. 1993. *Management for Productivity*. New York: Wiley.

The organizational context of decision making in government:

Brewer, Garry D. and Peter DeLeon. 1995. *The Foundations of Policy Analysis*. Homewood, IL: Dorsey Press.

Bryson, John M. and William D. Roering. 1987. Applying private-sector strategic planning in the public sector. *American Planning Association Journal*, Winter:9-22.

Fischer, Frank. 1995. *Evaluating Public Policy*. Chicago: Nelson-Hall.

Peters, B. Guy . 1995. *American Public Policy: Promise and Performance*, 4th ed. Chatham, NJ: Chatham.

Heineman, Robert A., William T. Bluhm, Steven A. Peterson, and Edward N. Kearney. 1990. *The World of the Policy Analyst: Rationality, Values, & Politics*. Chatham, NJ: Chatham.

Lindblom, Charles E. and Edward J. Woodhouse. 1993. *The Policy-Making Process*, 3rd ed. Englewood Cliffs, NJ: Prentice Hall.

Wilson, James Q. 1989. *Bureaucracy: What Government Agencies Do and Why They Do It*. New York: Basic Books.

Chapter One-A
PROBLEM DEFINITION
AND STRUCTURING

OBJECTIVES

After studying this chapter you should be able to

- define a problem concisely,

- distinguish individual elements of a decision problem: decisions, uncertain events, and objectives,

- structure a decision problem by representing the interrelationships among problem elements in an influence diagram,

- follow the structure of a decision problem represented by a decision tree.

The term *decision problem* refers to the combination of a problem to be resolved and a decision to be made regarding its resolution. The first step to solving a decision problem is defining the problem clearly. This chapter examines first the process of establishing an adequate problem statement, then the process of mapping the underlying *structure* of a decision problem, which indicates the various elements of the problem and their interrelationships. Once a clear picture of the overall structure has been developed, the analyst can focus on specific details, one at a time. This chapter presents two types of diagrams for representing the structure of a decision problem: influence diagrams and decision trees. The advantages of each diagram are discussed and step-by-step guidelines for creating an influence diagram from scratch are presented. Chapter One-B presents a shortcut technique for creating an influence diagram. Chapter One-C presents the procedure for solving some decision problems.

A computer-based decision support system can assist in developing, revising, and working with the structure of a decision problem. One such excellent system, DPL, was designed especially for decision analysis. Most of the illustrations in this book were created with this product. Appendix A provides a guide to its use. Alternatively, an analyst might use a spreadsheet for decision problems that are not too complicated. Instructions for using spreadsheets for decision analysis are provided in Appendix B.

DEFINING A PROBLEM

For purposes of decision analysis, a *problem* is operationally defined as the difference between a current and some preferred situation. Based on this definition, a well-formed problem statement should clearly indicate at least three components: the nature of the current situation, the nature of the preferred situation, and a central objective that distinguishes the two. There can be more than one basis for the preference, but there must be at least one.

A very common mistake in defining a problem is to prematurely focus on the alternatives. Quite often, a problem will be initially defined around whether a proposed alternative should be implemented. A key requirement for working with the rational model is patience. It is important to start by identifying the problem, the aspect of the current situation that needs improvement. Looking at the problem carefully, the analyst can identify what alternatives could help resolve the situation. These alternatives might represent a wide range of possibilities that have little in common except that they are all possible responses to the problem. Misdefining a decision problem as whether to implement a specific alternative, typically leads the analyst to focus on only those alternatives that strongly resemble the alternative initially considered.

Solutions in Search of a Problem: Some Examples
The following concerns are not expressed in the operational form of a problem:

- Should welfare recipients be fingerprinted?
- Should Gavin buy a new car?
- Should the XYZ ball-bearing manufacturing plant be closed down?
- Should there be a death penalty?

Each of these statements actually presents a solution in search of a problem. The answer to each depends on the ultimate objective. One way to start the search for the underlying problem is to ask why the proposed alternative is being considered.

Why should welfare recipients be fingerprinted?
Why should Gavin buy a new car?
Why should the XYZ plant be closed?
Why should some criminals be executed?

A problem statement should start by identifying the problem, not a possible solution. Here are better statements of the preceding concerns:

- Some people are receiving more than one welfare check.
- Gavin's car might break down at any time.
- The production costs at the XYZ ball-bearing plant are higher than at others.
- Unrepentant murderers are being released into society and committing further offenses.

These restated problems clearly imply what is the matter with the current situation and what situation would be preferred.

Widening the Decision Problem

Because problems are interconnected, it is often appropriate to expand the focus of a decision analysis beyond the initial concern. One way to determine whether a decision problem is sufficiently broad is to focus on the preferred situation indicated by the problem statement and identify all of the potential impediments to achieving it. These impediments can indicate which interconnected problems, if any, should also be addressed. Sometimes a problem is so inextricably associated with another that it is impractical to resolve it alone. For example, marriage counseling might fail if an individual does not receive help for alcohol abuse; improvements in product quality may not result in increased sales without an improvement in the company's image; increasing pollution controls might stifle a local economy unless coupled with a plan for economic development.

Quite often, an apparent problem is really the result of a deeper underlying problem. Hence, it is essential to ask why the problem exists in the first place. In each of the following case studies, a careful examination of the nature of the problem will substantially guide the subsequent analysis:

Identifying the Underlying Problem: The Crack Epidemic, Part I

Starting in the mid-1980s, abuse of crack cocaine presented a major problem in the United States. This problem can be described in terms of a comparison between a current and a preferred situation. As of the mid-1980s, many Americans were inhaling crack cocaine, resulting in deteriorating health, inter-personal problems, and crime. It would be preferable if no one smoked crack.

On the other hand, is crack smoking really the problem? Why do people abuse crack cocaine? Is it due to a breakdown of family relations? inadequate education? lack of employment opportunities? misinformation about long-term consequences? excessive peer pressure?

One opinion holds that crack abuse is not really a problem; rather, it is a symptom of other underlying problems. Crack abuse has called our attention to the fact that something is wrong, yet trying to resolve the crack problem directly might prove ineffective. Addressing the underlying problems might more productively help reduce the abuse of crack and other drugs.

Identifying the Underlying Problem: The Ball-Bearing Plant

Acme Industrial Products wondered why it cost more to produce ball bearings at the XYZ plant than at any of their other facilities. Is the equipment out of date? Are employee relations weak? Is the plant poorly managed? They proposed studying the problem for a week.

The answers to the questions they posed should suggest the most appropriate types of solutions. For example, if the problem is high production costs, there are several alternatives to closing the plant, including modernizing the facility, or marketing the product to users who need exceptionally durable ball bearings and are willing to pay more.

Limiting the Problem's Scope

After examining any underlying and connected problems, the problem statement might exceed what an analyst can reasonably address in the amount of time allotted. In this case, the analyst should try to limit the focus of the study. This might involve selecting a specific location or aspect of the larger problem. In general, the choice of the subproblem will be guided by the decision maker's priorities.

Limiting Problem Scope: Homelessness in Fallsburgh

The Red Ribbon Charities, a private philanthropy, is interested in the growing problem of homelessness in Fallsburgh. A preliminary study indicated the problem was associated with plant closings, drug abuse, and divorce. The study also indicated that there was more than one reason for homelessness and that there were different types of homeless people including single parents, the long-term unemployed, substance abusers, and former mental patients. Moreover, the problem was not restricted to Fallsburgh. Homelessness existed in neighboring counties and throughout the country.

To fully solve the problem appeared to involve remaking the social, political, economic, and education systems, perhaps throughout the country. Such a large task was well beyond the philanthropy's capability. Hence, the Red Ribbon Charities stuck with their general philosophy of providing relief to targeted groups in Fallsburgh, where they could make a difference. They chose to help homeless single parents in the inner city. They felt that this group was particularly needy because of their role in raising children, the future of the city.

Describing the Problem in Detail

An important part of the problem definition step is describing the details of the problem. Some details to consider in describing a problem include the following: How big is it? How many people are affected? How much money is involved? What caused the problem? When did it begin? What solutions have been tried? Why weren't they completely successful? Who else is interested in resolving the problem? What resources are available to solve the problem? A detailed understanding of the problem can be of great help in the subsequent steps of the decision analysis.

STRUCTURING A DECISION PROBLEM

How do you design a house? a computer? a car? Each of these complicated products contains numerous elements. Most importantly, in the end all of the elements must be properly connected for the final product to work. Similarly, decision problems contain numerous inter-connected elements. The basic approach to all of these design problems involves careful thought along three directions: the appearance of the final product, the details of each element, and the relationships between elements.

To design a car, a design team first identifies the car's essential characteristics based on its intended use. During this conceptualization, designers consider such issues as desired performance, overall capacity, durability, safety, fuel efficiency and cost. This vision in turn suggests some of the elements that should be included such as the engine size, the seating capacity, and the suspension system. Thus, design of the vehicle progresses to specifying the details of each of these subsystems.

The process, however, does not continue in such a straight-forward manner. The design of each element can have an impact on the design of another element. The fuel efficiency of the engine has an impact on the size of the gasoline tank. A more powerful engine might be less fuel efficient and, therefore, require a larger fuel tank to achieve a reasonable cruising range (the number of miles between refills). However, a larger fuel tank requires more room, which forces the designers to consider either less seating, less trunk space, or a bigger car. Hence, in the process of designing each of the vehicle's subsystems and their interrelationships, the designers might change their overall concept for the vehicle. Perhaps the overall specifications were overly restrictive. Maybe the vehicle will have to be more expensive in order to provide more performance, efficiency, and capacity. Alternatively, the concept might change to de-emphasize overall performance.

Just like designing a car, identifying the structure of a decision problem involves movement between thinking about the overall structure, details of individual elements, and their interactions. Decision problems include three types of elements: *decisions, uncertain events*, and *objectives*. This section describes each of these elements and how their interrelationships are represented in two types of diagrams: influence diagrams and decision trees. These representations provide a model of an analyst's understanding of a decision problem. The section proceeds to describe the step-by-step process of identifying the elements and their interrelationships, known as *structuring the decision problem*. This process can be greatly expedited by recognizing the overall structure up front. To this end, Chapter One-B presents several commonly prevailing types of decision problems.

Decisions. A *decision* is a choice between two or more alternatives. (If there is only one alternative, then there is no decision to be made.) By convention, a decision is represented as a rectangle, as illustrated below. The various alternatives are represented as branches stemming from the common decision point. Because of this branching, this representation is known as a tree diagram.

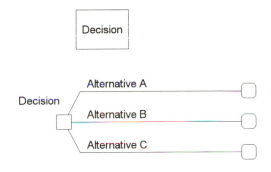

Decisions: Empire Remote Telephones, Part I

Empire Telephone recently developed technology that allows users to stray much further from their base units than with previous remote telephones and provides much clearer voice transmission. Empire Telephone has to decide upon an initial pricing strategy for the first year of sales. They could charge either $180 or $250 per unit. The marginal cost per unit was $120. Since research, development, and preparation of new production facilities had been expensive, they wanted to recoup as much money as possible through early sales of the product.

Uncertain Events. An *uncertain event* is a situation outside the control of the decision maker that could result in either of two or more possible outcomes. By convention, an uncertain event is represented as an oval, as illustrated below. The various possible outcomes are represented as branches stemming from the point of uncertainty. The integral structure of this element is the same as for a decision, a central point with alternative paths stemming from it. The difference between these elements is in who chooses which path will prevail. For a decision, a decision maker chooses the preferred path. For an uncertain event, forces beyond the decision maker's control determine the path.   A fully specified uncertain event identifies the probability of each possible outcome. Chapter Four, on forecasting, presents techniques for estimating such model inputs.

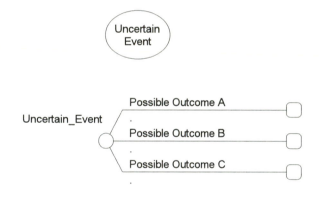

Uncertain Events: Empire Remote Telephones, Part II
An important element of Empire's decision problem is how well the product will sell. They cannot predict sales with certainty. It is not clear how many people will buy the product or what Empire's competitors might do. The sales of the product can be represented as an uncertain event. The following illustration shows an uncertain event labeled "Sales" and three possible sales outcomes, identified as low, medium, and high. Uncertain events can have as few as two possible outcomes or a virtually unlimited number. One possible outcome does not make any sense, because an event with only one possible outcome contains no uncertainty.

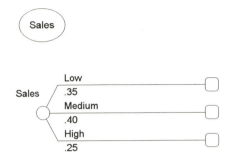

Choosing how many possible outcomes to associate with an uncertain event is a judgment call. A larger number of outcomes provides greater realism. However, each additional outcome adds to the complexity of the model, which increases the time that it takes to collect all the information necessary to complete the analysis. In general, it is advisable to choose a small number of possible outcomes (perhaps two or three) during initial model development.[4] Additional outcomes can always be considered later.

An influence diagram is a model of a decision problem. It does not have to be perfectly complete. It needs only to capture the essence of the decision problem. Chapter Four discusses the use of models further. Chapter Six revisits the question of whether the model is accurate enough or should be revised.

A fully specified uncertain event must indicate the probability of each possible outcome. The figure above reports marketing's best guess at the possibility of various sales figures: 35% chance of high sales, 40% chance of medium sales, and 25% chance of low sales. These initial estimates are based on a retail price of $250.

Objectives. An *objective* is a criterion for evaluating the desirability of a situation. By convention, objectives are represented as rectangles with rounded corners as illustrated below:

---

[4]DPL also allows the user to specify outcomes of uncertain events as continuous distributions, taking on all values over a range. In the high-frequency telephone case, actual sales could be modeled as ranging anywhere from $0 to $100 million. This book, however, restricts itself to the use of a limited number of discrete possible outcomes for ease of specification, use, and presentation.

For many decisions, simply maximizing total profits is of such overwhelming importance that no other objectives need to be considered. In contrast, public policy problems are often characterized by a large number of objectives.

Objectives: Empire Remote Telephones, Part III
Empire's primary concern is to make as much money as possible. However, when it comes to introducing new products, other strategic concerns come into play, such as obtaining market share of an emerging product line, developing a reputation as providing prestigious products, and providing a full line of products. These elements can be expressed as objectives, as follows:

Influence Diagrams

Influence diagrams present a high-level view of the relationship between decision elements. By convention, these diagrams are expressed chronologically from left to right as illustrated in the typical influence diagram below. Most often, the diagram starts with a *primary decision*, a choice to be made now, at the far left. Which alternative is chosen may affect the probabilities associated with the various outcomes for a subsequent uncertain event. Such a relationship is illustrated by an influence arrow from the primary decision to the uncertain event. The direction of the influence arrow indicates the direction of influence from the decision to the uncertain event. The results of uncertain events occurring at time 1 may be taken into consideration in making a subsequent decision. The figure illustrates two uncertain events—one influenced by the primary decision and one that is not—affecting a subsequent decision by connecting influence arrows.

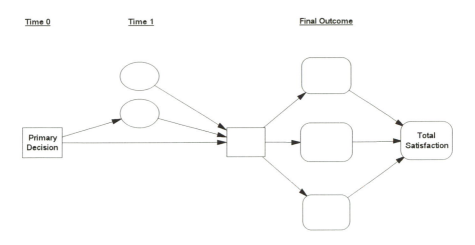

Time 0   Time 1   Final Outcome

The width of an influence diagram represents the *planning horizon*, the length of time into the future considered in the analysis. The right side of the diagram, after all the decisions and uncertain events have occurred, represents the *final outcome* or state of the world prevailing at the end of the planning horizon. The ultimate goal is to maximize the decision maker's overall happiness as represented by a total satisfaction node at the far right of the diagram. The figure indicates that there are several objectives, vertically arrayed, that have an influence on total satisfaction. This type of decision is therefore referred to as a *multi-objective* decision problem. In such problems, decisions and uncertain events directly influence the various objectives, but not total satisfaction. Total satisfaction is fully determined only by how well the final outcome scores on each of the objectives specified.

Decision Trees

Decision trees provide a detailed representation of all the paths that may prevail within a decision problem's planning horizon according to the alternatives associated with each decision and possible outcomes associated with each uncertain event. Like influence diagrams, they are read from left to right. The figure below illustrates a typical decision tree:

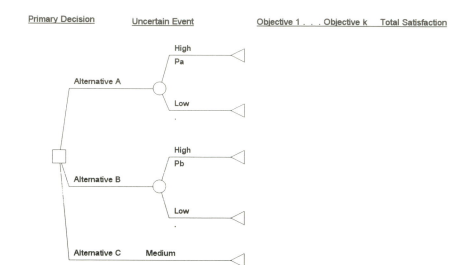

A decision tree can be thought of as a type of a trail map. Each line represents a trail segment to be traversed. Each point of interconnection, known as a *node*, indicates where any of several paths might be chosen. For a typical decision problem, the root of the tree at the far left is the primary decision. In the decision tree illustrated above, the decision maker can follow one of three alternatives paths. Subsequently, the decision maker faces an uncertain event. The probability of a high outcome, the upper path, is affected by the alternative chosen at the time of the primary decision. If alternative A is chosen, the probability of the high outcome is P_a. If the high outcome does not occur, then a low outcome prevails. If alternative B is chosen, the probability of the high outcome is P_b. If alternative C is chosen, then the uncertainty is eliminated and a medium outcome automatically prevails. Hence, the circle indicating branches of an uncertain event is not included along the pathway at the bottom of the diagram.

The right of the diagram represents the final outcome. Each endpoint at the right of the diagram corresponds to the end of a distinct path through the various decisions and uncertain events of the problem. These endpoints are called *final outcomes*. The numbers at the end, known as a payoff matrix or scorecard, provide an evaluation of each final outcome according to each objective included in the problem. (Chapter Four discusses procedures for estimating probabilities and payoffs.) The last column provides the value for total satisfaction for each final outcome.

One problem with decision trees is that their size increases exponentially with the complexity of the problem. For example, adding a subsequent decision with three possible alternatives to the figure above, after the uncertain event, increases the number of final outcomes from five to fifteen. The expression "decision trees can get bushy" summarizes this concern.

Influence diagrams are much less cumbersome to work with. The problem just presented as a decision tree can be represented in an influence diagram with one decision, one uncertain event, and $k + 1$ objectives, for a total of $k + 3$ elements. The addition of another decision increases the number of elements to $k + 4$, a very modest change in complexity. For this reason, influence diagrams are particularly useful for initially conceptualizing the structure of a decision problem.

Structuring from Scratch

This section presents one approach to creating an influence diagram. One of the most difficult tasks in structuring a decision problem is confronting a blank sheet of paper (or the blank screen when entering DPL). Of note, writers and painters also remark on the difficulty in getting started. Advanced preparation can reduce this anxiety. A first step to structuring a problem is to simply list the various decisions, uncertain events, and objectives involved in the decision problem. This step is easier than approaching the entire decision problem because it avoids identifying the influences and details, which complicate matters. Furthermore, these lists do not have to be exhaustive since there will be ample opportunity to add elements later on. Next, these lists should be roughly rank ordered from the most central elements to the least.

Structuring a decision problem can be likened to assembling a jig-saw puzzle. Once the key elements have been identified, one can start to piece them together. A good place to start is by connecting the primary decision to a single objective. The next step is to enter the most elementary version of the decision problem. Every decision problem must have at least one decision; otherwise there is no opportunity for the decision maker to resolve the problem. Every decision problem must also have at least one objective; otherwise it does not matter which alternative is selected. If there are multiple objectives, label the initial objective "total satisfaction."

Subsequently, elements are added or spliced into this diagram one at a time, roughly in the order in which they appear in the lists. For extensive problems, this process can be greatly aided by use of computer software, such as DPL. Throughout this process, the need for additional elements not on the original lists may become apparent. On the other hand, as the process proceeds, some of the elements that were on the list may not seem so important. In this case, they can be left out of the influence diagram.

Which elements should be included in any decision problem is a judgment call. Once the original lists of elements have been exhausted, the influence diagram as a whole should be carefully examined. At this time it can also be helpful to ask others to evaluate how closely the model resembles their understanding of the problem.

To recap, the steps to structuring a problem from scratch are as follows:

Steps to Structuring a Decision Problem from Scratch
1. Create three lists: decisions, uncertain events, objectives,
2. Sort lists in decreasing order of importance,
3. Create initial influence diagram: decision ⟹ objective,
4. Add elements one at a time until initial lists are exhausted,
5. Evaluate the overall structure, and revise if necessary,
6. Ask others to evaluate the overall structure, and revise if necessary.

Structuring from Scratch: Empire Remote Telephones, Part IV
Empire's decision problem includes the following elements:

Decisions	Uncertain Events	Objectives
Price	Sales	Profit
		Market Share
		Reputation
		Complete Product Line

The initial influence diagram presented below captures the essence of the problem–the choice of the price somehow affects Empire's satisfaction. In particular, a higher price means more profits for a given amount of sales.

However, sales is an unknown factor. Moreover, the price of the telephone will affect sales. Thus, the next element to add to the diagram is the uncertain event of sales. An influence arrow points from price to sales indicating, that price affects sales, and an arrow points from sales to total satisfaction, indicating the influence of one on the other.

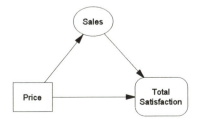

The only elements left to enter are the objectives. These will essentially be spliced in between the arrows leading into total satisfaction, since decisions and uncertain events do not directly affect total satisfaction in a properly structured diagram. Price and sales both clearly affect profit. Market share is affected by sales, but not directly by price. Price's influence on market share is only through its influence on sales. Reputation is affected by price. A low price will help the company's reputation as providing good value to the customer. Neither price nor sales affects the size of the company's product line. Therefore, this last objective can be excluded from this decision analysis. The following figure illustrates the final model of Empire's decision problem:

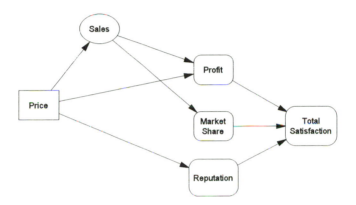

That's it for elements. Does the representation make sense? The diagram indicates that the price Empire sets on its new remote telephone will affect sales of the product. The sales of the product in combination with its price affects total profits. There are also two strategic objectives included in the analysis: Empire's market share, which is affected by the new phone's sales, and the company's reputation for providing value, which is affected by price. Empire's total satisfaction is a function of how much profit it makes, its market share, and its reputation.

❏ SUMMARY

A problem can be operationally defined as the difference between a current and a preferred situation. In a well-formed problem statement, at least three components should be distinguishable: the nature of the current situation, the nature of the preferred situation, and a central objective that distinguishes the two. The current and preferred situations may differ according to more than one objective.

A decision problem includes various elements that can be identified as decisions, uncertain events, and objectives. The interrelationship among these various elements can be illustrated in an influence diagram, which presents influence arrows indicating which elements affect others. A decision problem can also be represented as a decision tree, a series of branches indicating the potential alternatives that can be chosen and outcomes that may occur in order of time precedence from left to right.

☐ EXERCISES

1. The following concerns are not expressed as properly formed problem statements. Identify a possible underlying problem that could have led to each concern. Provide a properly formed problem statement for each concern that identifies the current situation and why some other situation would be preferred.

    a. Should Daily BreadCo lease their delivery trucks?
    b. Should Route 17 be expanded into a six-lane highway?
    c. Should Gavin start a savings account for retirement?
    d. Should ABC publishing open a hypermedia division?
    e. Should there be a 10:00 p.m. curfew for people under the age of 18?
    f. Should Bill be promoted to assistant manager?
    g. Should Kwang buy a cat?
    h. Should Springfield open a free family counseling clinic?
    i. Should Dexter Photo Finishing run an advertisement during the Super Bowl?

2. Kim Strum recently underwent back surgery. Unfortunately, she has ended up in greater pain after the surgery than before. She sued her surgeon for $5 million. If she wins in court, her lawyer assures her that she will receive the full $5 million, but if she loses she will receive nothing. The doctor's insurance company, APS Professional Insurance, prefers to avoid going to court, when possible. Consequently, they have offered Kim $1 million to settle the case out of court. Structure Kim's problem using an influence diagram.

3. Dry Gulch receives most of its water supply from several reservoirs upstate. Until recently, the city's water purity was excellent, because the land surrounding the reservoirs was mostly undeveloped. Unfortunately, in recent years the quality of the water has declined. In order to insure a continued supply of high-quality water, the city could install a filtration system. This solution would be quite expensive. Alternatively, the city could continue to block development in the upstate areas surrounding the reservoirs. Residents of the upstate communities have complained that these restrictions are unfairly hurting their economy. Given the recent spate of corporations that have reduced the size of their workforce, stimulating economic growth is an important concern. Structure Dry Gulch's problem using an influence diagram. (Hint: not all decision problems include all three types of decision elements.)

4. Decision trees and influence diagrams are alternative methods of representing decision problems. Describe the difference between them. Explain the advantages of each method.

☐ FOR YOUR PROJECT

1. Create three lists of problem elements: decisions, uncertain events, objectives. These lists should be as extensive as possible. Use your judgment to rank the elements in each list from the most essential to the least.

2. Structure your decision problem as an influence diagram. If your diagram becomes particularly complicated please stop and postpone further work. It may be much easier to continue after studying Chapter One-B, which presents shortcut techniques for identifying the structure of a decision problem.

Chapter One-B
COMMON DECISION STRUCTURES

OBJECTIVES
After studying this chapter you should be able to

■ examine a new decision problem and quickly identify its structure as essentially conforming to one of several common types.

Many decision problems have a similar structure, even though the problem context may be completely different. This chapter presents several basic structures that occur quite frequently. Knowing these structures helps a decision analyst quickly identify the structure of a new decision problem.

BASIC RISKY DECISION

Many problems revolve around making a choice in the face of uncertainty. In the basic risky decision, illustrated below, the decision maker's satisfaction is a function of both the choice made and the outcome of an uncertain event.

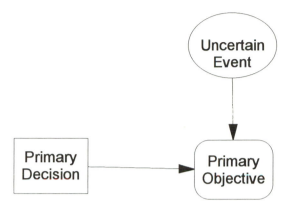

Basic Risky Decision: Venkat's Lemonade Stand

Venkat is considering opening a lemonade stand at the beach this summer. When swimming and relaxing in the sun, people enjoy a cool refreshing drink. If it's a particularly hot summer, Venkat could earn a lot of money. However, if it rains a lot, sales will suffer.

This decision problem can be succinctly illustrated with three elements: a decision as to whether to open the lemonade stand, an uncertain event regarding the amount of rain, and a primary objective of making money. Whether Venkat opens his stand and how much it rains will determine his profits. This relationship is illustrated in the influence diagram below.

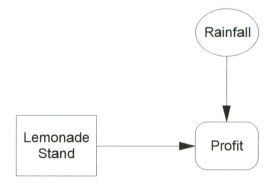

This basic structure can describe many investment decisions. For example, it describes a decision to open a new franchise, create a new product, or start a new service, regardless of what the franchise, product, or service might provide. The success of each of these ventures typically depends on the uncertain event of sales. The basic risky decision can also describe decisions as to whether to purchase insurance. In the risky investment problem, the analyst decides whether to become involved in a venture that entails risk. In the insurance decision, the analyst currently faces a possible risk and decides whether to reduce any potential loss by purchasing insurance.

Basic Risky Decision: Life Insurance
Donna has been wondering how much life insurance she should buy—perhaps none. If she has no life insurance, her untimely death would leave her family financially distressed. Life insurance guarantees income to her family, irrespective of her mortality. On the other hand, the more life insurance she buys the more she has to pay. In this problem, the decision is how much insurance to buy, the uncertain event is Donna's mortality, and the objective is her family's financial security.

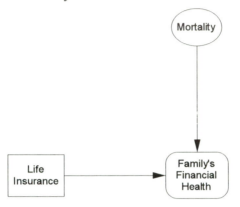

Insurance not only refers to the purchase of a paper policy; many activities are commonly performed to help insure against disaster. For example, wearing a seat belt may be inconvenient, but in case of an accident it will help insure a passenger's safety. Thus, the basic risky decision can be used to describe how various operating decisions insure against an undesirable result.

Basic Risky Decision: Tomato Harvest
Assan needs to decide when to harvest his late-season tomatoes. His goal is to have as large a crop (measured in pounds) as possible. Hence, he wants to leave his tomatoes on the vine as long as possible, perhaps until the end of September, so that they will be their plumpest and ripest. On the other hand, starting in September there is a risk of frost. If Assan has not harvested before the frost hits, he loses his entire late-season crop. In this problem, the decision is when to harvest the tomatoes, the uncertain event is the date of the first frost, and the objective is to maximize the tomato yield. Both Assan's decision as to when to harvest and the weather affect the eventual yield from the crop as illustrated below:

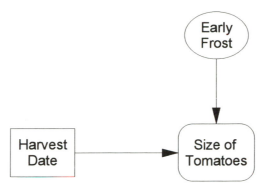

BASIC RISKY POLICY

In some problems, the alternative selected has an influence on the probabilities of the possible outcomes associated with the uncertain event. The simplest such model, the basic risky policy depicted below, involves just three elements: primary decision, uncertain event, and objective.

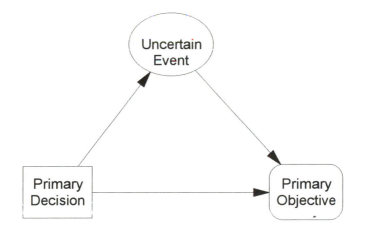

Basic Risky Policy: A Help-Line for LawAccounts, Part I

LawAccounts sells a computer program that supports the accounting function for small law partnerships. To make their product more attractive they are considering offering a help-line to provide perpetual free customer support. Introducing this feature should greatly improve sales. However, providing the service is very expensive and will eat into profits.

In this problem, both the decision (to offer a Help-Line) and the uncertain event (sales) influence profits. But unlike in the basic risky decision, the uncertain event (sales) will be affected by the primary decision. The structure of this decision problem is illustrated below.

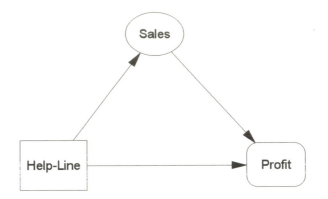

BASIC RISKY DECISION WITH MULTIPLE OBJECTIVES

Often, insuring against one risk results in forgoing some other desirable opportunity. In this case, the additional opportunity can be modeled as a second objective. Determining the best solution involves making a tradeoff between the objectives.

The figure below illustrates a basic risky decision with more than one objective. In such a problem, each objective might be influenced by the primary decision, the uncertain event, or both. The importance of each objective is subsequently evaluated in terms of how it affects total satisfaction. A modest variation of this model occurs when the primary decision influences the uncertain event. Such a problem is referred to as the basic risky policy with multiple objectives.

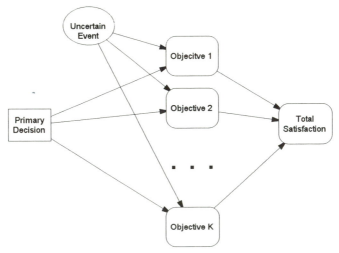

Basic Risky Policy with Multiple Objectives: A Visit to Colombia
The vice president of a large engineering firm is planning a trip to Colombia to present a proposal for the development of a new airport. Given a history of corporate kidnapings, security is on his mind. He has considered several security plans that differ primarily by the number of bodyguards involved. The more bodyguards, the lower his risk of being kidnaped, but the more expensive the program. The following influence diagram illustrates his problem:

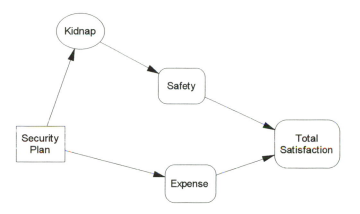

MULTIPLE-OBJECTIVE, NO-RISK DECISION

In some problems, the tradeoff between various objectives is paramount and risk is not a major issue. This structure often occurs in public policy problems in which a tradeoff among the objectives of various stakeholders must be determined, as illustrated below. The final decision affects a variety of objectives, each of which affects total satisfaction.

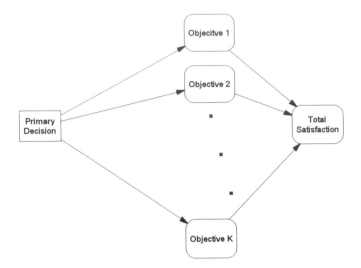

Multiple-Objective, No-Risk Decision: Leaf Composting

The town of Greenburgh prides itself on the abundance of trees within the community. On the down side, when the trees lose their leaves each fall a substantial waste problem results. Until recently, the leaves were collected and brought to a local nursery, which composted them into topsoil. Last year, a controversy arose as residents living near the nursery complained about the smell and asked that composting be prohibited within town limits.

The town's primary decision, to allow or prohibit commercial composting, affects many of the town's objectives. Prohibiting composting would improve residential aesthetics. However, it would also add to municipal expense to cart and dump the leaves elsewhere, restrict business opportunities, and force jobs out of the community. The town of Greenburgh is in the unenviable position of making a ruling: unenviable, because no alternative simultaneously eliminates the smell, saves money, stimulates business, and creates jobs. The final decision will represent a tradeoff among these various concerns. The following figure illustrates this problem:

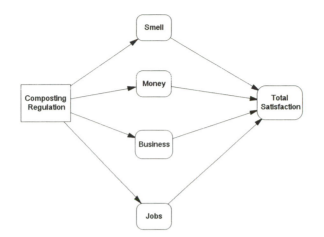

MULTIPLE-OBJECTIVE, MULTIPLE-APPROACH, NO-RISK DECISION

Some policy problems are so broad and complicated that a single program would not resolve it completely. Some examples of such problems include drug abuse, violence, crime, unemployment, and homelessness in the public sector. For a business, the problems of organization morale, new product identification, and efficiency may also be too large to resolve with a single approach. The range of options and the elements germane to each of these decisions are so large that developing a single decision model to represent the problem becomes too complicated.   A general approach to such problems, called *hierarchical decomposition* involves dividing the problem into more manageable subproblems. The decision structure then becomes twofold: deciding on how much emphasis should be placed on solving each subproblem, and choosing a course of action for resolving each subproblem. The relative importance of each subproblem is often expressed by how much of the budget is allocated to each.

Multiple-Objective, Multiple-Approach, No-Risk Decision: U.S. Drug Policy

In 1988, President George Bush established the Office of National Drug Control Policy to provide central oversight and coordination in the war against drug abuse. Each year, the Office provides a statement of the nation's current drug control strategy, which serves as the basis for the president's budget proposal to Congress.

The 1994 policy states that no single solution appears to be adequate for controlling drug abuse; rather, a combination of approaches aimed at restricting the availability of illegal drugs and simultaneously reducing the popularity of drugs was deemed the best approach. Accordingly, the budget provides financing to a variety of solutions including treatment, education, community action, workplace prevention, policing, international relations, interdiction at borders, research, and intelligence.

A central budget request for $13 billion divided among the programs indicates the relative importance of each. The 1994 budget request placed additional emphasis over previous years on reducing the demand for drugs, especially among frequent cocaine users, by increasing funding of drug treatment. The plan also outlines approaches to be pursued within each program. For example, the statement emphasized source country interdiction with cooperative South American countries as opposed to border patrols.

MULTIPLE-PERIOD SEQUENTIAL DECISION

Often a decision maker does not have to lock into an alternative once and forever. Conditions may change and suggest discontinuing a program that previously was deemed useful, or implementing a program that previously did not appear to be necessary. The central structure of this problem is a series of basic risky decisions in successive time periods with influence arrows between them indicating how the problems are linked, as illustrated in the figure below. The decision in one time period affects satisfaction in the same time period. The decision also affects prevailing conditions and the nature of what type of decision needs to be made in the next time period. The outcome of an uncertain event in one time period influences total satisfaction in that time period and provides important information affecting the decision in the next time period. Total satisfaction over all time is influenced by satisfaction within each time period.

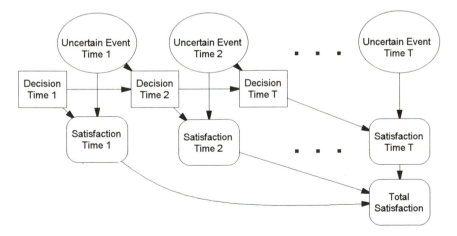

The power of this representation lies within the explicit recognition of the links between decisions. The opportunity to change at a future date often suggests that a riskier alternative in the present time period could be pursued. If negative consequences result, a more conservative strategy could be implemented in the future. Alternatively, the opportunity to change at a future date could provide the basis for deferring a decision until a more auspicious opportunity presents itself.

Multiple-Period Sequential Decision: Hypermedia, Part II
The hypermedia problem involves two linked decisions, to implement a hypermedia division in 1996, and to implement a hypermedia division in 1998. The influence diagram below illustrates these two decisions and indicates the time sequence of the decisions with an influence arrow. The uncertain event, hypermedia use in 1998, influences both satisfaction in the first time period and which alternative seems most profitable in the second. The 1996 decision influences profits from 1996 to 1998.

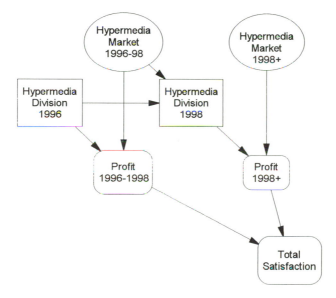

The 1998 decision influences profits beyond 1998. Profits from 1996 to 1998 and profits beyond 1998 both influence total satisfaction. This total satisfaction allows the analyst to specify the relative importance of immediate profit to future profit. This decision structure could be straightforwardly modified to specify reevaluating development of a hypermedia division every two years after 1998.

PROTOTYPE DECISION

For large-scale projects, it often pays to consider implementing a smaller version first, known as a *prototype*, involving a smaller initial commitment. Most importantly, the information obtained through experiences with the prototype can help reduce much of the uncertainty concerning whether a larger version would be successful. On the other hand, spending time developing and observing a prototype delays the day when definitive action is taken to try and resolve the problem. The following influence diagram illustrates this multiperiod decision problem:

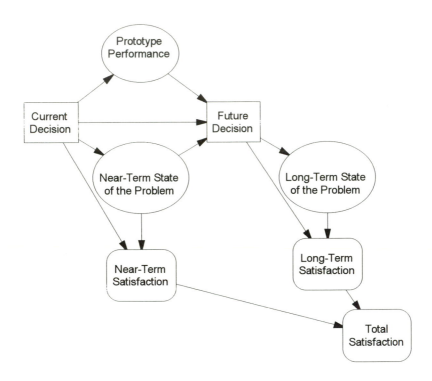

Prototype Decision: Community Policing
The City of Belleville's police department is considering implementing a program of community policing in an effort to reduce their continually high crime rate. Community policing requires officers to be proactively involved in the reduction of crime-related problems within a community in addition to their existing responsibilities.

The City could implement community policing citywide. Alternatively, they are considering starting slowly by implementing the program in a few precincts as a demonstration program to learn more about the program's effectiveness and to see if it is worth the expense. The following influence diagram indicates how running a demonstration program this year provides additional information to inform the decision next year. However, by postponing the broader implementation of community policing the city forgoes any current benefit.

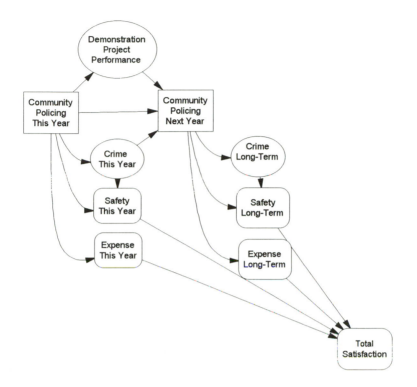

□ SUMMARY

Determining the detailed structure of a decision problem can be difficult. However, identifying a similarity between a decision problem and common decision structures can greatly facilitate this process. Some common decision structures include basic risky decision, basic risky policy, basic risky decision with multiple objectives, multiple-objective no-risk decision, multiple-objective, multiple-policy, no-risk decision, multiple-period sequential decision, and prototype decision.

□ EXERCISES

Develop influence diagrams to describe the following decision problems:

1. The Loon Society recently asked the Landmark Hotel to serve as the site for their national conference. Naturally, since they would guarantee that they would fill the hotel, they asked for a 30% discount off the usual rates. The Hotel wasn't sure what to do. If they were lucky, and the hotel was filled with regular guests on that weekend, they'd earn more money than the Loon Society was willing to pay. However, this meeting represented a guaranteed income.

2. Kumar is purchasing a new home and needs to decide how to finance it. He can choose between a fixed thirty-year mortgage and pay 8% interest or choose an adjustable mortgage. The current interest rate on the adjustable mortgage is 7%. Kumar could save a lot of money if interest rates stay about the same. However, if rates go up, he could end up paying as much as 10%.

3. Recently, the Cross-Town Moving Company went out of business. Because they owed back taxes, the town of Dunford took ownership of their lakefront warehouse. The town is considering what to do with it. The facility could be sold to be used as a warehouse again, which would provide tax revenue. Alternatively, it could be turned into a park, which would provide recreation for the town residents.

4. In the last five years, Siam House has grown into a successful restaurant. The owners feel that the popularity of Thai cuisine is growing and will continue to increase. Consequently, they are considering opening a second restaurant on the other side of town. However, they are uncertain the current demand could support a second restaurant. Alternatively, they could wait until next year or the year after to make a decision.

5. Sommerville is planning to build a swimming pool this fall. It will be completed in time for use next summer and will provide a center for community activity, especially for youths. They are considering three possible sites, each of which is attractive for different reasons. The Main Street site seems attractive because it is centrally located. However, it is also the most expensive. The Wood Street site is quite scenic. The Jefferson Street site, although located on the outskirts of town, is the largest, thus providing room for future expansion.

6. State University has become concerned about the growing number of sophomores who are poor writers. Some members of the curriculum committee have suggested a two-semester freshman writing fundamentals course be required. This alternative is somewhat unpopular because it reduces the number of free electives that allow students and faculty to explore more advanced topics. Another alternative is to open a writing laboratory where students could voluntarily bring their term papers and receive extra help. However, the students who need the most help might not be the ones to avail themselves of this service. One thought is that they could implement the writing lab for a year and see how well it does. If it doesn't work out, then they could always add the two-semester writing course.

7. Notchville is planning a sesquicentennial celebration for Saturday, June 17, six months from now. Activities will include marching bands, picnicking, and family games. However, they are concerned about the possibility of rain. They consulted the almanac, which indicated only a 10% chance, which is quite low. Still, if it did rain, the party would be ruined. As a backup, they could rent space at the convention center. However, the convention center will charge $10,000 for booking the facility whether the city uses it or not.

8. Ashok recently fell seriously ill after eating a meal he had prepared at home. He announced that he first started feeling faint after eating some mushrooms. A police lab did find traces of cyanide in an open can of MC mushrooms back at his house.

   MC Mushrooms Corporation was both angry and concerned. Someone had tampered with their product. It might have been back at the plant, in which case other cans could have been affected. Alternatively, Ashok or someone else in his home could have planted the cyanide in their product. Irrespective of the reason, MC Mushrooms has to respond and soon. They could recall all of their mushrooms and destroy them, they could recall those packed on the same day as the can associated with the incident, or they could decide not to have any recall. The more extensive the recall, the greater the expense, but the less the likelihood of another incident. Another incident would force them to have a total recall and would hurt the company's reputation, a second objective in resolving this decision problem.

9. Due to increased use of air transportation for freight, many shipping piers have fallen into disuse. Anchor Incorporated is considering purchasing Pier 27, which is conveniently located, and developing it as a recreational facility. They are considering either tennis courts, an indoor play space for children, or a swimming pool. As a business, they really don't care much about which service they provide, only how much profit they can expect to earn. Of course, the success of the venture depends on an uncertain public reaction.

10. Intelligence reports indicate that an extremist group has stockpiled an extensive array of illegal firearms. The Bureau of Alcohol, Tobacco, and Firearms [ATF] has determined that this group poses a serious threat to the security of the area and has maintained an armed guard around the group's compound. No one has gone in or out for the last 45 days.

    The head of operations has become concerned and is considering taking further action. She wishes to minimize the loss of life both among members of the extremist group and among her own officers. Naturally, her total satisfaction with the outcome will be some unequal combination of these two objectives. If they continue this siege, the militants will eventually run out of food and surrender. However, it is estimated that surrender will not occur until after a quarter of the members have starved. Alternatively, they could storm the compound and take the members by force. If the element of surprise works, there will be no loss of life. However, if an armed conflict ensues it is expected that half of the militants and four ATF officers would die.

11. Robberies of senior citizens have increased dramatically in the Brownstone section of the city. The police are considering adding patrols in this area. This would surely reduce crime, but it would be expensive. Furthermore, the heightened police presence would create additional tension with inner-city minority youths, many of whom feel victimized by the police. Alternatively, they could implement a much less expensive, neighborhood watch program. Moreover, this would create a sense of community involvement. However, a community watch program may or may not reduce the crime problem. Finally, they could simply maintain their current level of police patrols.

12.   Self-elected benefits represent a major trend in compensation planning. Kwamee works for the Omega Corporation, which allows employees to contribute to a 401k savings plan for long-term savings, earmarked for use in retirement. This plan is quite popular since every dollar an employee contributes is matched by an additional 50 cents from the company, providing up to an additional 5% of an employee's salary. This money can be invested in either the fixed interest account with a guaranteed interest rate of 6.5% or in Vanguard Index 500, a broad-based stock fund.

Kwamee, who is currently thirty-five years old, would like to have as much money at retirement as possible. The 6.5% interest rate sounds fine, much better than money market rates offered by his bank. However, stock funds historically have earned closer to 15%, although past performance is no guarantee of future earnings. In fact, Kwamee is skeptical about the stock market and suspects that stocks might be drastically overvalued. He estimates from current price-earnings ratios that if companies continue to perform about as well as they are doing now he can expect a 3% return.

13.   Brighton's public officials have not received a pay increase in several years. Many career civil servants are complaining. Whereas their cost of living in the city has increased, their income has not kept pace. The city is particularly concerned since it recognizes the importance of maintaining morale. Furthermore, many contend that adequate salaries are essential for attracting qualified individuals into public service.

The city council is considering two possible pay raises. The first would establish a basis for the raises through salary comparisons to competitive labor markets prevailing in industry. Under this plan, subsequent raises would be keyed to raises occurring in the private sector. This approach seems fair, although it would be very expensive. Alternatively, the city could simply increase salaries by 20%, across the board.

Many elected individuals and citizens are against any pay raise. They argue that the city's financial problems are paramount. Hence, the city simply cannot afford salary increases. They further argue that low salaries are good. They argue that people who enter public service in spite of the modest salaries tend to be highly committed individuals.

14.   With the growth of genetic engineering, the AIDS epidemic, and the environmental movement, many people are becoming concerned with their diet and turning to organically grown foods. Consolidated Foods produces a wide variety of canned goods in high volume, available primarily through large supermarket chains. In order to capitalize on the current interest, they are examining the potential for producing organic tomatoes, peas, and corn, their best selling products. However, food fads come and go. If they enter the organic food business and demand shifts, they could face major losses. The risk is particularly high because it takes seven years of chemical-free cultivation before a field can be certified as organic.

15. The CEO of Solutions Incorporated was accused by his secretary of making unwelcome sexual advances. The CEO did make sexual overtures; however, it is not clear whether the secretary had consented. Hence, there is only a modest 20% probability that a court would rule in favor of the secretary. On the other hand, if they do, it could cost the company as much as $1.5 million and they would be forced to fire the CEO in order to maintain their corporate reputation. They would like to keep the CEO because he has been an effective manager. Alternatively, they could settle the case out of court for $600,000.

16. Greensman Home Products manufactures a variety of gardening equipment including lawn mowers, hedge trimmers, chain saws, and edgers. Ronald, the vice president of manufacturing has been reading about how quality circles can improve corporate productivity. Quality circles involve holding weekly meetings with the production staff to discuss ways of improving coordination, cooperation, and product quality. Thus, the company must pay for two hours of work per week during which employees are not directly producing anything, which could result in a 5% decline in output. On the other hand, the journal articles suggest that improved cooperation and quality consciousness could result in as much as a 50% increase in output. Ronald could implement quality circles throughout the company. Alternatively, he could develop a quality circle for their hedge trimmer operation, see how productivity changes, and then consider implementing them more broadly after a year.

☐ FOR YOUR PROJECT

1. Identify which common model structure most clearly describes the nature of your decision problem and explain why. If necessary, revise the representation of your decision problem accordingly.

Chapter One-C
SOLVING DECISION PROBLEMS
BY MAXIMIZING EMV

OBJECTIVES

After studying this chapter you should be able to

- convert an influence diagram into a decision tree,

- solve a decision problem that has the single objective of maximizing money.

This chapter introduces how to identify the "best" solution to a decision problem based on the criterion of *maximizing expected monetary value* [EMV], that is to identify the course of action that on average yields the most money. This criterion is most appropriate for decision problems in which money is the only objective and the risks are not overly large.

For many problems, this criterion is inappropriate. However, the procedure used for solving problems with extensive risk and/or multiple objectives is simply a modification of the procedure for maximizing EMV. In these problems, the analyst first defines an index of total satisfaction to summarize how each final outcome fares across the various objectives. (This material is covered in Chapter Five.) Subsequently, the analyst identifies the alternative that maximizes this index using the same procedure introduced in this chapter for maximizing EMV.

The procedure for maximizing EMV is straightforward when a decision problem is represented in a decision tree. Therefore, this chapter starts by describing how to convert an influence diagram into a decision tree. For an influence diagram, the analogous calculation is more complicated to perform by hand. (Of course, if the influence diagram is created using computer software such as DPL, the program will perform the computations.)

INFLUENCE DIAGRAM TO DECISION TREE CONVERSION

Converting an influence diagram into a decision tree is straightforward. (Converting a decision tree into an influence diagram is more complicated and is not covered in this book.) The procedure involves trimming the influence diagram, while growing the decision tree, one node at a time as follows:

Procedure for Converting an Influence Diagram into a Decision Tree
1. IDENTIFY THE LEFTMOST ELEMENT OF THE INFLUENCE DIAGRAM: Select a decision or uncertain event on the far left of the diagram that has no influence arrows pointing to it. If there is more than one such element, choose any one of them. This element represents the first event to occur. Quite often, this node will be the primary decision. In the influence diagram depicted below, the primary decision on the left side at the bottom of the figure is the first event to occur.

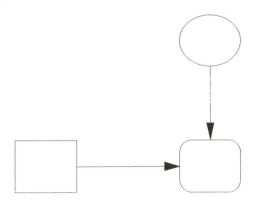

2. DRAW NODE IN DECISION TREE: Create a node in the decision tree corresponding to the element identified in the previous step. If the element is a decision, create a branch emanating from the node for each alternative. If the element is an uncertain event, create a branch emanating from the node for each possible outcome. Indicate the probability of each possible outcome on the branch.

3.   DELETE ELEMENT FROM INFLUENCE DIAGRAM: Delete the element
       from the influence diagram corresponding to the node added to the decision
       tree. Delete influence arrows emanating from the removed element.

4.   CHOOSE NEXT ELEMENT FROM INFLUENCE DIAGRAM: Identify
       the leftmost decision or uncertain event with no influence arrows pointing
       to it; this is the next event to occur. (This step is essentially the same as
       step 1.) In the diagram above, the next element is the uncertain event at the
       top.

5.   DRAW NODES IN DECISION TREE: Draw a node on the end of each
       branch at the far right of the current decision tree.   Draw a branch
       emanating from each of the new nodes for each alternative or possible
       outcome associated with the decision element. For uncertain events, enter
       the probability of occurrence on each branch.

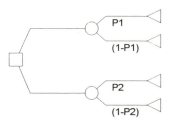

6.   DELETE ELEMENT FROM INFLUENCE DIAGRAM: Delete the element from the influence diagram that corresponds to the node just added to the decision tree. Delete any influence arrows that were emanating from the element. The diagram below illustrates that deleting the last uncertain event left only the objective.

7.   REPEAT STEPS 4–6: Continue to delete decisions and uncertain events from the influence diagram and add them to the decision tree, until there are no more left.

8.   ENTER PAYOFFS: Enter the payoffs associated with each objective into a scorecard at the end of the decision tree.

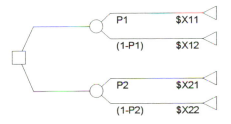

Converting to a Decision Tree: A Help-Line for LawAccounts, Part II
The following influence diagram specifying the decision problem for LawAccounts can be straightforwardly converted to a decision tree.

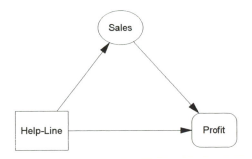

The first step is to create a node in the decision tree for LawAccount's primary decision, whether to open a help-line, and remove this node from the influence diagram.

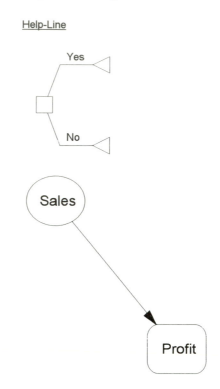

Help-Line

Yes

No

Sales

Profit

The next step is to represent the uncertain event, sales, in the decision tree.

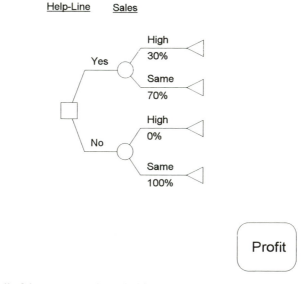

Help-Line   Sales

Yes

High
30%

Same
70%

No

High
0%

Same
100%

Profit

Now that all of the events are included in the decision node, the profit associated with each final outcome can be entered. LawAccounts hired a consultant to do a market analysis, which suggested that there was a good chance that LawAccounts could virtually double their business by adding a help line. The precise numbers are presented in the following decision tree.

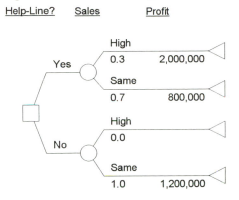

In this case, the uncertain event on the lower branch is unnecessary, because sales will certainly stay the same if LawAccounts does not change its service. Removing this uncertainty yields the following decision tree:

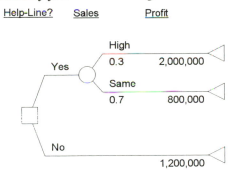

SOLVING PROBLEMS BY MAXIMIZING EMV

The general rule for solving a decision problem is to select the "best" alternative. This criterion appears quite reasonable; however, it is not always easy to identify what is meant by best–particularly for problems involving risk and multiple objectives. This section presents a series of successively more complicated decision problems to illustrate how a best alternative is determined. All of these problems have a single objective, maximizing money.

When analyzing decisions that involve money, it is important to be aware of when the payment occurs. A thousand dollars received next year is not worth as much as a thousand dollars received today. In particular, $944 invested today at an interest rate of 6% would be worth $1,000 a year from now. In this sense,

$1,000 next year is equivalent to or is said to have a *net present value* [NPV] of $944, assuming an interest rate of 6%. It is standard practice, in decision making, to convert all payments (whether to be received or paid) into their equivalent worth today or NPV. Appendix D reviews procedures and issues involved in calculated NPVs.

The No-Risk Decision Problem. When a problem involves no risk and a single objective, such as money, the best alternative is obviously the one that scores highest on that criterion. For a sales decision, this involves choosing the opportunity that results in the greatest income. Similarly, for a purchasing decision, it is best to choose the supplier charging the lowest price. In both these cases, the decision maker is maximizing monetary value. The solution procedure is to choose the alternative associated with the largest income (or smallest cost).

The No-Risk Decision Problem: Choosing a Rivet Supplier
Ketina Jones is in charge of ordering supplies for Associated Airplanes Manufacturing. Recently, the company that provided their rivets went out of business, leaving her to identify a new supplier. She received bids from three companies large enough to supply Associated's need on an ongoing basis. Based on a volume discount, Central Steel Products said they would charge $275 per case, United Manufacturing Supplies said they would charge $285, and American Rivet Products said they would charge $265. Ketina decided to order her rivets from American Rivet Products because they had the lowest price. The following decision tree illustrates Ketina's problem and the solution:

The Basic Risky Decision Problem. One procedure for solving single-criterion decision problems involving risk is to *maximize expected monetary value* by substituting the EMV for situations in which the outcome is uncertain and choosing the alternative with the largest EMV. For example, consider a choice between two alternatives, A and B, as illustrated below. The payoff associated with alternative A is known with certainty. Alternative B is a risky proposition with a 50% chance of providing $10,000 and a 50% chance for $50,000. The criterion of maximizing EMV suggests assuming this alternative is worth $30,000, the average of the two outcomes.

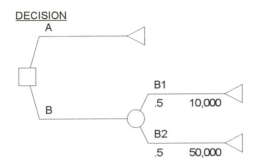

On the one hand, this substitution seems eminently reasonable and logical. The payoff associated with alternative B must be reduced to a single number so that it can be compared with alternative A. Moreover, that number should be less than $50,000, which is the maximum payoff that might not occur. That number should also be greater than $10,000, since that represents a minimum guaranteed payoff. Thus, halfway in between, or $30,000, seems like a reasonable value to associate with alternative B.

On the other hand, there is something disconcerting about this substitution. Under no circumstance will alternative B result in a payoff of $30,000. It will either result in substantially more, $50,000, or substantially less, $10,000. In this sense, the expected payoff seems like an odd construction.

Often in decision making, maximizing EMV makes good sense, especially in the long run. The *franchise problem* illustrates this perspective. A business that generates income in one location–a restaurant, cleaning service, entertainment center, or retail outlet–will often be successful in another. Of course, establishing a business is expensive and there is no guarantee of success. The figure below illustrates the decision of whether to establish a business with a 10% chance of a $10,000,000 payoff, a 70% chance of a $1,000,000 payoff, and a 20% chance of losing the initial stake of $3,000,000. All dollar values have been converted into their NPV for ease of comparison.

Franchise

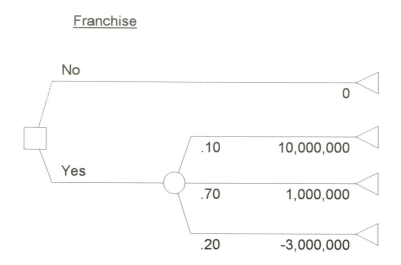

Such franchising decisions are made frequently. In fact, let's assume that this company is deciding whether to simultaneously open franchises in 100 different locations and that the risks and potential rewards are similar at each. If all 100 sites were opened, clearly some would be very successful, and others moderately successful, and some would almost assuredly be losers. In fact, 10 big winners would be expected (10% of 100 franchises), 70 moderately successful franchises would be expected, and 20 franchises would be expected to be failures. In this case, total profit can be determined as the sum across the individual franchises, as follows:

$10,000,000   + $10,000,000   + . . . (10 times) . . . + $10,000,000 +
$ 1,000,000   + $ 1,000,000   + . . . (70 times) . . . + $ 1,000,000 -
$ 3,000,000   - $ 3,000,000   - . . . (20 times) . . . - $ 3,000,000

= 10 × $10,000,000 + 70 × $1,000,000 - 20 × $3,000,000

= $100,000,000 + $70,000,000 - $60,000,000

= $110,000,000 or an average of $1,100,000 per franchise

Overall, the decision to open the 100 franchises would be a good idea because it would probably enrich the corporation by $110,000,000, even though some franchises are successes and others are failures. Moreover, the answer to each of the 100 individual franchise decisions is to go ahead with it. On average, each opportunity can be expected to contribute $1,100,000 to the company.

This same long-run logic is encapsulated in the criterion of maximizing EMV. The EMV of an alternative is equal to the probability of each possible outcome multiplied by the payoff associated with it, summed across all possible outcomes, as represented in the following formula:

$$EMV[x] = p_1 \times x_1 + p_2 \times x_2 + \ldots + p_K \times x_K$$

Where,

p_k = the probability of outcome k
x_k = the monetary payoff associated with outcome k
K = the number of outcomes associated with uncertain event, x

In one sense, EMV can be viewed as a weighted average of all possible outcomes where the weights are the probabilities of each outcome. Alternatively, EMV can be viewed as the expected contribution per decision when a similar decision is repeated many times. The EMV for the franchise example illustrates this point:

$$EMV = .10 \times \$10,000,000 + .70 \times \$1,000,000 + .20 \times (-\$3,000,000)$$

$$= \$1,000,000 + \$700,000 - \$600,000$$

$$= \$1,100,000$$

The structure of this calculation for EMV is identical to the calculation of the average contribution per franchise previously presented. Hence, both the EMV and the average contribution are $1,100,000.

Maximizing EMV: Milo's Homemade Ice-Cream, Part II

Milo now runs a chain of forty-five successful premium ice cream stores in the northeastern United States. Business has been so successful that Milo is considering opening as many as twelve more stores.

He was initially concerned about the fact that he might actually lose money at some of these locations. However, he contented himself by the fact that if most of the stores are successful then he will be way ahead of the game. Consequently, he decided to use the principle of maximizing his EMV to decide how many and which locations to open. Using his business plans and assuming a ten-year operating horizon he calculated the net present value of profits for each location based on a best-, medium-, and worst-case scenario for the store. These dollar values (in millions) and the probability of each scenario are presented below:

Location 1

	NPV	Prob.
Best	$2	20%
Medium	$1	50%
Worst	-$1	30%

EMV: $.6

Location 2

	NPV	Prob.
Best	$4	40%
Medium	$1	40%
Worst	-$1	20%

EMV: $1.8

Location 3

	NPV	Prob.
Best	$2	20%
Medium	$1	40%
Worst	-$3	40%

EMV: -$.4

Location 4

	NPV	Prob.
Best	$1	40%
Medium	$.5	40%
Worst	-$1	20%

EMV: $.4

Location 5

	NPV	Prob.
Best	$3	40%
Medium	$2	40%
Worst	$.5	20%

EMV: $2.1

Location 6

	NPV	Prob.
Best	$2.5	20%
Medium	$1.5	40%
Worst	-$.5	40%

EMV: $.9

Location 7

	NPV	Prob.
Best	$1.5	40%
Medium	$1	50%
Worst	-$3	10%

EMV: $.8

Location 8

	NPV	Prob.
Best	$2	20%
Medium	$.5	40%
Worst	-$2	40%

EMV: -$.2

Location 9

	NPV	Prob.
Best	$3.5	20%
Medium	$1	50%
Worst	-$1	30%

EMV: $.9

Location 10

	NPV	Prob.
Best	$4	20%
Medium	$2	50%
Worst	$1	30%

EMV: $2.1

Location 11

	NPV	Prob.
Best	$5	30%
Medium	$1	40%
Worst	-$3	30%

EMV: $1

Location 12

	NPV	Prob.
Best	$1.5	10%
Medium	$.5	30%
Worst	-$1	60%

EMV: -$.3

Based on this analysis he opened shops at all the locations with a positive EMV, which excluded locations 3, 8, and 12. The EMV of the total expansion was $10.6 million.

Complicated Decision Problems. The way to solve a complicated decision problem involving numerous decisions and/or uncertain events is to reduce it to the no-risk decision problem. The procedure works on the decision tree representation, one node at a time, from right to left. First, a node at the far right of the diagram (one with no successors) is reduced to a single number, its EMV. For decisions, this involves selecting the best alternative. For uncertain events, this involves averaging across all possible outcomes. Each such replacement reduces the size of the diagram, which eventually exposes every node in the decision tree. The procedure continues until only one element, the primary decision, remains. At this point, the diagram resembles the no-risk, single-criterion decision problem and the best alternative is the one associated with the largest EMV.

Solving Complicated Decision Problems: A Cure for Lyme Disease, Part I
The pharmaceutical business can be highly lucrative, especially when one finds a cure for a previously incurable disease. Jackson Pharmaceuticals Inc. is considering funding a research team to find a cure for Lyme disease. Bill MacKenzie, the executive vice president of research, must ultimately make this decision.

The research program has a total price tag of $10 million and there is no guarantee that it will be successful. In fact, Bill estimates only a 40% chance that they will find a cure. If the research team finds a cure, Jackson Pharmaceuticals must then decide whether they wish to produce the drug themselves or sell the license to a chemical lab for $40 million. (All payoffs are net present values but exclude the cost of performing the research.) If they produce the product themselves and production goes smoothly, they forecast a $60 million payoff. But refitting one of their production facilities can be troublesome. There is a 30% chance of production troubles, in which case they would only earn $20 million.

The following decision tree illustrates this decision problem:

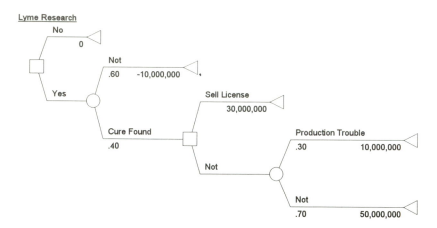

The diagram shows that Jackson Pharmaceuticals knows how much money they will make if they do not invest in Lyme disease research. To determine whether they should invest depends on how much they expect to make if they do invest in Lyme disease research. However, their expected payoff depends on whether they would produce the drug themselves or license someone else to do it, if they found a cure. Hence, this contingent decision must be resolved first.

To solve this decision tree, Bill MacKenzie reduced each decision element to a single number, from right to left. He started by calculating the EMV associated with the uncertain event, production trouble:

$$.30 \times \$10,000,000 + .70 \times \$50,000,000 = \$38,000,000$$

The revised decision tree looked as follows:

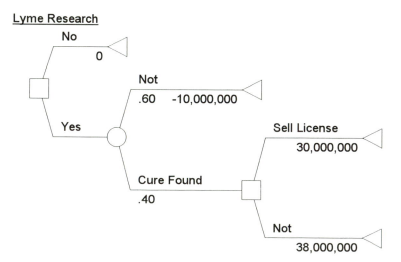

Next he considered whether they would sell the license for the cure. In spite of the possibility of production trouble, the EMV for producing the drug themselves was higher than the amount they could get for a license. So, Bill made the subsidiary decision that Jackson Pharmaceuticals would produce the Lyme disease cure themselves, given the opportunity. The revised decision tree looked as follows:

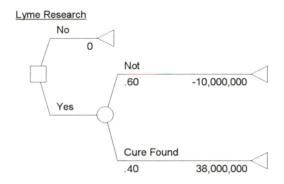

Next he averaged the expected payoff over the probability that a cure is found:

$$.60 \times (-\$10,000,000) + .40 \times \$38,000,000 = \$9,200,000$$

This left him with values for EMV associated with each alternative of his primary decision.

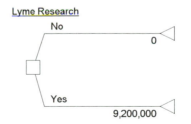

The EMV associated with initiating Lyme disease research was substantial, in spite of high startup costs and uncertainty. Consequently, Bill MacKenzie recommended that Jackson Pharmaceuticals start such a program.

The following steps summarize the procedure for solving a decision problem using the criterion of maximizing EMV. This procedure assumes that the decision problem is represented as a decision tree.

Steps to Solving a Decision Tree

1. IDENTIFY A RIGHTMOST NODE: Select a node that does not precede any other nodes. These are typically located at the far right of the diagram. Such a node represents one of the last events to occur within the planning horizon.

2. DETERMINE THE EMV ASSOCIATED WITH THE NODE: Determine the expected payoff at this point in the decision tree. Decisions and uncertain events are evaluated differently.

    a. IF THE NODE REPRESENTS A DECISION: Choose the alternative with the largest EMV.

    b. IF THE NODE REPRESENTS AN UNCERTAIN EVENT: Average the payoff across the various possible outcomes using the following formula:

    $$EMV[x] = p_1 \times x_1 + p_2 \times x_2 + \ldots + p_k \times x_k$$

3. REPLACE THE NODE WITH ITS EMV: Remove the node and its associated branches from the decision tree and insert the EMV just determined in its place. Alternatively, the EMV can be written above the node and all of the branches to the right of it disregarded.

4. RETURN TO STEP 1: Continue folding back the decision tree according to the previous steps until the diagram has been completely analyzed and a best alternative to the primary decision has been determined.

☐ SUMMARY

For many decision problems, the best alternative is the one that maximizes the expected monetary value. These problems typically involve only money as an objective and do not involve excessive risk. The folding-back procedure for determining a best alternative is to evaluate each element in a decision tree from right to left. This entails averaging payoffs across all possible outcomes for uncertain events and choosing the best alternative for each decision.

☐ EXERCISES

Solve the following decision problems using the criterion of maximizing EMV:

1. The Department of Public Works for the City of Snowdon is preparing for winter. One concern is having enough salt on hand to keep the roads clear. Their current Fall shipment costs $50,000 and is usually enough. However, about one in every five years they run out. These heavier winters require 30% more salt. If the City purchases the extra salt at the beginning of the year, it will cost an additional $15,000. However, if the city waits for a possible emergency shipment in the middle of the winter it will cost double. Create a decision tree that describes Snowdon's

inventory problem. (Hint: It may be helpful to first create an influence diagram and then convert it to a decision tree.) What do you recommend?

2. The Lemon Grove Citrus Company is faced with its annual late-season harvest question. Should they harvest their late season crop or let it grow for an extra month? If they harvest early, the crop will bring in $1.2 million. If they wait, however, the late season fruit yields a higher price, resulting in sales of $1.4 million. Of course, there is a 25% chance of frost. If a frost occurs, then the fruit will be completely ruined. Create a decision tree to describe this decision problem. What should Lemon Grove Citrus Company do? What if the probability of frost were 35%? or 10%?

3. Computer Systems Incorporated is starting a new division to provide accounting programs to small companies. One question that arose is whether to hire programmers as full-time employees or to obtain long-term contractors from a temporary services agency. Based on their experience, they feel that contract employees provide the same levels of technical ability and professionalism as full-time employees. So they are not concerned about their work. It is really only a question of money. Typically, full-time employees are cheaper. They could develop the initial product for $480,000. Contract labor would cost $600,000.

    However, there is one important reason for using contract labor. When the project is over, they go somewhere else. If full-time employees are hired, then they can expect continued employment. If the initial project is unsuccessful (and it is estimated that there is only a 40% chance of success), Computer Systems Incorporated will close the new division. If the division is closed, the software developers will need to be terminated and outplaced. Total outplacement expense for the staff is estimated at $180,000. Create a decision tree that describes this human resources decision. Make a recommendation as to how Computer Systems Incorporated should proceed.

4. The Main Street bridge in the town of Lincoln is starting to wear. A civil engineering firm estimated that it would cost $600,000 to repair it. The engineers warned that if they delayed for a year and further erosion occurred the repair work would cost $900,000. Given that a mild winter is expected, and based on the condition of the bridge, they estimated this probability to be 35%. Most importantly, however, they assured the city manager that in spite of the further structural damage the bridge would not pose a safety hazard.

The city manager would like to delay the renovation for one year, because there is a 60% chance that the town will receive $300,000 in matching funds from the state. If the funds are not granted next year, then there is still a 45% chance they will be granted the year after. In this case the town could delay the repairs again, unless the bridge has deteriorated, in which case it must be fixed. If they postpone repairs, the town again risks a 35% chance of further damage. Create a decision tree to describe this infrastructure maintenance problem. What would you recommend the town do?

5. The Ectron Fragrance Corporation is considering producing a new fragrance named Action, designed for youthful, athletic women. This is a fairly risky proposition, since this group as a whole does not tend to use fragrance regularly. The marketing department has forecasted three possible scenarios: (A) the product could create a whole new market among women who were not loyal to any other fragrance, leading to profits of $17.5 million over a three-year planning horizon; (B) the product could develop a satisfied following, providing profits of $2.8 million; or (C) athletic women who are not fragrance oriented could avoid the product completely, resulting in losses of $3.2 million. (Note: Losses should be represented as a negative number in your representation of the decision problem.) Their initial probability estimates for the likelihood of each scenario are as follows: $P_A = .10$, $P_B = .40$, $P_C = .50$.

    Due to the product's inherent risk, marketing is considering the option of first releasing the product in a small market and seeing how well it sells. However, the test marketing itself costs $750,000, and would thus reduce the product's potential profitability. Marketing estimates that the probability that the product will be well-received in test marketing efforts is 70%. If they run the test market and the product is well-received, then the forecasts for the product's success are as follows: $P_A = .30$, $P_B = .60$, $P_C = .10$. If the product is not successful in the test market, the forecasts are as follows: $P_A = .04$, $P_B = .26$, $P_C = .70$. Create a decision tree which describes the Action Fragrance decision. Make a recommendation as to how Ectron should proceed.

6. Hobie Jennings designed a new children's computer game, "Let's Build a House," which he has personally promoted to computer and children's stores. Sales so far have been good, he's moved over 2,000 units, and he's learned how to promote the product more effectively. If sales continue along the same trend, he estimates he'll probably sell a total of 10,000 units.

    However, there is a 20% chance that the game will really catch on. In this case Hobie would expect to move 100,000 units. On the other hand, there's a 10% chance that sales have already peaked and he'll sell a total of only 3,000 units. Hobie clears $6 on each unit sold after marketing and production expenses. You can assume this margin remains constant, regardless of the number of units sold.

Recently, Hobie was approached by Mega Software Enterprises. Mega would market the game using their distribution and promotional channels and pay Hobie $3 on each unit sold. Mega is really big. Hobie estimates there is a 30% chance that the game will sell 100,000 units for them. Moreover, Mega has a 10% chance of selling 200,000 units. If the game is not a hit, Mega expects to sell 10,000. Mega knows that Hobie is eager to see income and has prepared an alternative proposal. They would pay $50,000 for the rights to the game, and $1 for each unit sold.

Hobie was very flattered by the offers, but wondered if he needs to make a decision now. He decided that he could possibly wait for one year; by that time he would have sold as many units as he possibly could on his own. If the product did not sell 100,000 units, there's still a 60% chance that Mega would still be interested in marketing it. However, their deal would be $2 per each additional unit sold. Mega's chance of selling an additional 90,000 units would be 10%, an additional 5,000 would be 70%, and no additional units 20%. Prepare a decision tree to describe this marketing problem. What action do you suggest for Hobie? (For this exercise you should disregard the time value of money and other nonmonetary objectives.)

Identify the alternative which maximizes EMV:

7.

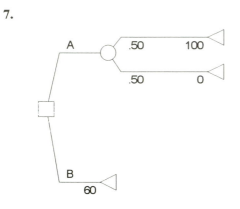

8.

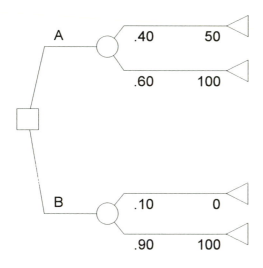

9.

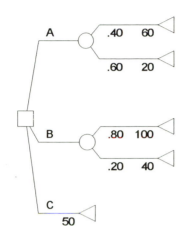

10.

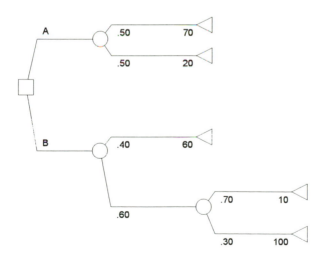

11.

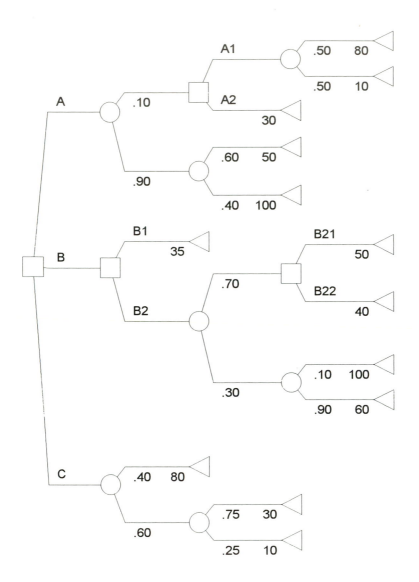

12.

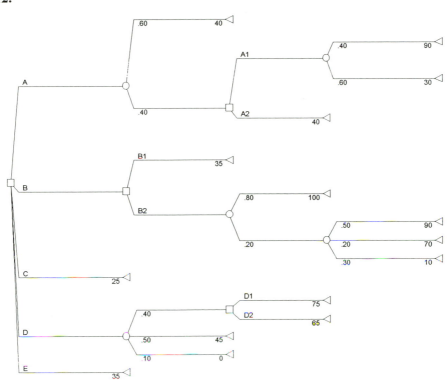

Chapter Two
IDENTIFYING OBJECTIVES
AND CREATING A VALUE TREE

OBJECTIVES

After studying this chapter you should be able to

- distinguish between an objective and a means to an end,

- prepare a comprehensive, orderly list of objectives associated with a problem.

Decision analysis involves both mathematical calculations that are carried out in a precise, objective manner and value-laden comparisons that are inherently subjective. The objectives included in an analysis represent the decision maker's values, or the values of the group of people the decision maker represents. In this regard, if the analysis were performed for a different decision maker, the objectives included as essential to the analysis could differ. Most importantly, the priority associated with each value often differs across decision makers. Identifying the priority associated with each objective is covered in Chapter Five. This Chapter examines the process of comprehensively identifying objectives and organizing them into categories. This stuctured list of objectives is called a *value tree*. Before techniques for identifying objectives are presented, the structure of a value tree is examined.

For many decision problems, particularly in business, the exclusive objective is to maximize profits through increased revenue or reduced costs. In these cases, the procedure for maximizing the expected monetary value presented in Chapter One-C is most appropriate. Public policy and strategic planning decisions almost always include concerns about numerous objectives.

Identifying Objectives: Relocating Alpha Brokerage Services, Part I
Alpha Brokerage Services is considering moving its headquarters from
Manhattan to suburban New Jersey. Financially, the move sounds promising.
The sale of the downtown facility would provide a major cash infusion in excess
of the cost of a new facility and property taxes would be lower. On the other
hand, there are additional expenses associated with moving, including relocating
staff, changing forms, and notifying customers.

Additionally, there are numerous considerations that are difficult to put a
price on but must be included in the analysis. Manhattan is a major financial
center. Hence, the location facilitates interaction with other financial
organizations, attracts new employees who already work in Manhattan, and
helps attract and retain customers who expect a brokerage company to be located
in Manhattan.

STRUCTURE OF A VALUE TREE

A value tree identifies how to evaluate the desirability of each final outcome. It
appears on the right side of an influence diagram, at the end of the planning
horizon, after all the decisions and uncertain events have occurred. The figure
below illustrates the format of a comprehensive value tree. This tree includes three
columns of objectives all eventually converging into total satisfaction. In practice,
not all multi-objective decision problems will use all four columns.

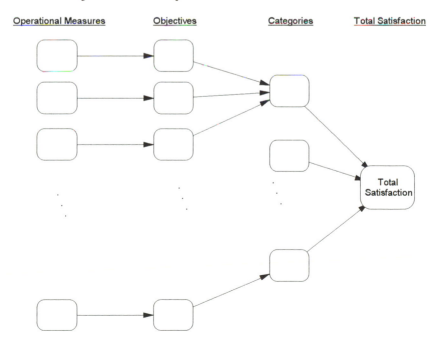

A Comprehensive Value Tree

At the core of the comprehensive value tree are the objectives that identify the decision maker's concerns, such as maintaining morale, being environmentally sensitive, or improving public image. These are the reasons why the problem is an important one to address. The columns on either side of the objectives, operational measures and categories, help in the process of evaluating how well each final outcome scores according to each objective and how important each objective is to the decision maker's total satisfaction, respectively.

In some decision problems, the objectives are difficult to measure because they represent broad concepts. How does one measure corporate morale? What exactly does it mean to be environmentally friendly? For such problems, it is often useful to specify precisely how each objective will be appraised. For example, employee turnover could be used to measure corporate morale, or average emissions used to measure environmental friendliness. These methods used to assess the final outcome are called *operational measures*.

Some decision problems include a mind-boggling number of objectives. Identifying similar concerns as part of larger, general categories of concern can help to organize the representation of objectives. For example, the objectives of employee morale, absenteeism, and benefits might all be grouped together into the general category of concerns regarding human resources in a decision problem.

The comprehensive value tree presented above illustrates the detailed logic of determining total satisfaction associated with any final outcome. First, the observable characteristics of each final outcome are identified as operational measures. Typically, these values can be directly identified from a forecast. (Chapter Four presents a discussion of forecasting.) Next, the value on each operational measure is subjectively evaluated as either a relatively good or bad level. (Chapter Five presents techniques for evaluating how one possible outcome compares to another on any scale.) Subsequently, the performance evaluation on the objectives are combined to determine how each final outcome performs in each general category. Lastly, the decision analyst identifies an overall score for each outcome based on the relative importance of each general category. (Chapter Five presents techniques for combining scores into general categories and into total satisfaction in detail.)

Value Tree: Buying a Clothes Washer

Consumer Reports provides rational buying advice for common household products on an ongoing basis. In preparing their recommendations, they identify several key features that determine a product's usefulness. The following value tree for selecting a clothes washer was derived from a report appearing in the February 1995 issue, on pages 96–101.

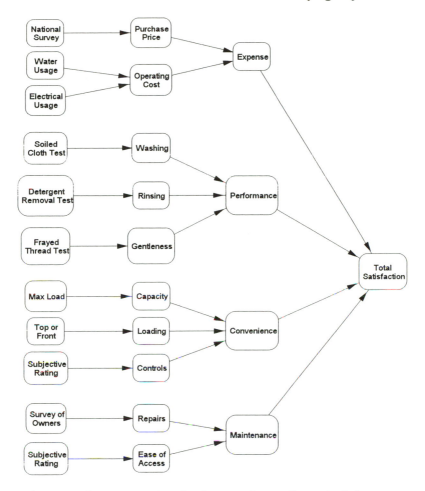

The general concerns when buying a major appliance include expense, performance, convenience, and maintenance. These comprise the general categories in the value tree illustrated above. Each of the specific objectives identified in the report can be classified into one of these four groups. Consumers Union is extremely conscientious about performing a scientific test of each objective, whenever possible. The results of these operational measures provide the basis for their product ratings.

IDENTIFYING OBJECTIVES

To develop a value tree, an analyst can start by making a list of all the objectives to consider. Usually, it is good to involve the decision maker at this point. The first objective to consider is the almost universal objective of money, either saving it or earning it. Money isn't always the most important objective in an analysis, however, it is almost always a consideration. In the business domain, earning and/or saving money is often the primary and sometimes the only objective. In the governmental domain, fiscal responsibility is nearly always an important consideration.

To find other objectives one must continually ponder the question, "Why does anyone care about this problem?" In order to obtain a comprehensive list of objectives, it might be useful to identify all the stakeholders affected by the decision problem and think about each one's special interests. (Note: This activity in effect implements the political model of decision making presented in Chapter Zero.) A recommendation will tend to draw wider support if it is explicitly sensitive to everyone's concerns.   Creating such a list is a relatively noncontroversial activity. The real conflict occurs at the comparison phase of the analysis (see Chapter Five), when the relative importance of each objective must be identified.

To obtain well-formed objectives, it is important to distinguish between concerns that are really means to an end and underlying objectives. *Means to an end* are goals that seem desirable. *Underlying objectives* are the values which make a goal seem worthwhile.

When asked about their objectives, quite often a group of stakeholders will say they are advocating a particular alternative. This answer indicates "what" they want but not "why" they want it.   Such statements are means to an end. Underlying objectives identify why. The tendency to identify means to an end instead of objectives is the essentially the same mistake as identifying a possible solution instead of defining the problem, as discussed in Chapter One-A. The stakeholders can be pressed to explain further with the question, "Why do you want that?" Sometimes this will elicit an underlying objective. Sometimes the stakeholders will present another means to an end, in which case the analyst might probe further. One way to know when an underlying objective has been found is when the answer to the question "Why do you want that?" seems obvious.

An analysis will be better informed if the underlying objective(s) can be determined. Understanding everyone's objectives can help an analyst identify ways to modify existing alternatives to help satisfy all stakeholders.

Identifying Objectives: Widening Maple Street

The town of Lincoln is considering widening Maple Street from two lanes to four. This project involves much expense, including purchasing the additional land and building the road. Furthermore, the additional roadway must be maintained over time, creating future maintenance expenses.

Various groups are interested in the situation. In general, the taxpayers within the community would like to keep building and maintenance to a minimum so as to minimize taxes. However, the financial considerations need to be weighed against broader community issues, such as fewer traffic jams and improved traffic safety. A nearby mall is very interested in the road expansion, because it would make the mall more accessible and increase its business.

When the street widening was first announced, the Maple Street Residents Association was formed to block it. They wanted to maintain Maple Street as a two-lane road. Hence, they stated that keeping Maple Street as a two-lane road was their objective. However, there is something funny about this objective. It doesn't tell us anything about the Maple Street Residents. In fact, this objective is really a statement about which alternative these stakeholders prefer and not about why it is preferred.

The Residents Association was asked to clarify why they objected to a four-lane road. Their initial response was that they want a two-lane road because they want to maintain a nice community. When pressed to explain what characterized a "nice community" they said they wanted a good-looking street, one that was safe for their children, and one that was quiet. This information could prove particularly useful for designing a solution to the problem. The best alternative might involve widening the street. However, based on these expressed concerns, trees might be planted along the side of the road and stop signs installed in order to better meet the residents' objectives.

The objectives identified for this decision problem quite naturally fall into three categories: Financial, Traffic Flow, and Local Concerns. These general categories and objectives are presented in the following value tree:

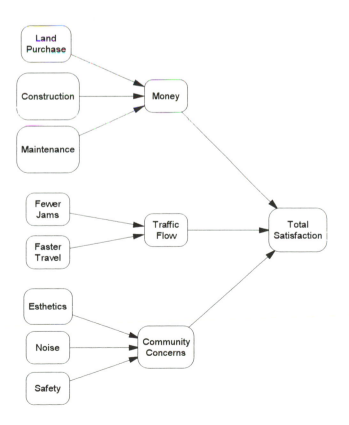

CREATING A VALUE TREE

If the list of objectives becomes large (more than four concerns), it is often useful to identify general categories. There are two general approaches to this task: top-down and bottom-up. The top-down approach involves identifying several general domains of concern based upon a basic understanding of the problem and then placing the objectives into these categories. The bottom-up approach involves identifying pairs or clusters of attributes as related, combining them into larger groups, and then determining an appropriate name for each such category. Typically, a justification for why each group is related tends to emerge while the groups are being created and serves as a category title.

The ultimate goal is to combine objectives into two to four general categories. Having a small number of general concerns helps in thinking about the essential tradeoffs of the problem. Finally, it is often useful to identify a way to operationally measure each objective, although for objectives that are particularly difficult to measure an operational measure is not always needed. Chapter Five discusses dealing with these difficult-to-measure concerns, further.

The procedure for developing a value tree is summarized as follows:

Steps to Creating a Value Tree

1. Start a list of objectives and place "save money" at the top. If the money involved is not important, then remove it from the list.

2. Ask "Why does anyone care about this problem?" To obtain a broad list of objectives, it might be useful to consider the various stakeholders affected by the problem and their concerns.

3. Distinguish between underlying objectives and means to an end by continually asking, "But why does anyone care about that objective?"

4. Return to step 2, until no more values can be identified.

5. Group objectives into two to four categories of similar values.

6. Optionally, identify operational measures of each objective.

☐ SUMMARY

Objectives guide decision analysis at every step of the rational process. Hence, a comprehensive set of well-formed objectives is essential. Such a set of concerns will almost always include money. For some decision problems, money is the only concern. One technique for developing a comprehensive list of objectives is to identify the interests of all stakeholders involved with the problem. Well-formed objectives can be distinguished from means to an end by asking the question, "Why does the stakeholder care about the stated objective?" Underlying values require no additional clarification.

For problems with numerous objectives, it is useful to organize them into a value tree. In a value tree, all of the objectives are grouped into two to four general categories of similar objectives. A value tree might also include one or more operational measures for each objective that specify how to assess how well each final outcome performs on each objective.

☐ EXERCISES

1. An important skill is the ability to differentiate between a means to an end and an underlying objective. Identify a possible value behind the following means to an end by asking why anyone would consider each of these concerns as important:

   a. Our goal is to expand our product line of kitchen tools.
   b. Politicians should not be in office too long.
   c. The potholes on Main Street need to be fixed.

2. Choose an article from *Consumer Reports* and create a value tree for buying a product based on the information.

3. Create a value tree for the following decision problems:

   a. Choosing a home, apartment, or living arrangement.
   b. Developing a corporate charity (such as Ronald McDonald House).
   c. Controlling drug abuse.
   d. Selecting a college.
   e. Choosing a movie for a date.
   f. Planning activities for a company picnic.

4. Several scholars contend that the essential tradeoff on issues of public policy comes down to favoring the interests of equality versus providing the greatest individual liberty, which can alternatively be characterized as public versus private interests, or democracy versus capitalism (Heineman et al., 1990, pp. 68-90; Schlesinger, 1986). Choose a problem in the public domain and create a list of objectives for consideration. Test the extent to which the theory holds by trying to group all of the objectives into one of two general categories, equality and liberty.

☐ FOR YOUR PROJECT:

1. Create a value tree for your decision problem.

☐ FOR ADDITIONAL INFORMATION ON

Identifying values:

Keeney, Ralph L. 1992. Value-Focused Thinking: A Path to Creative Decisionmaking. Cambridge, MA: Harvard.
Saaty, Thomas L. 1990. Decision Making for Leaders. Pittsburgh, PA: RWS.

Values in public policy:

Heineman, Robert A., William T. Bluhm, Steven A. Peterson, and Edward N. Kearney. 1990. *The World of the Policy Analyst: Rationality, Values, & Politics*. Chatham, NJ: Chatham.
Schlesinger, Arthur M., Jr. 1986. *Cycles in American History*. Boston: Houghton Mifflin.

Chapter Three
IDENTIFYING ALTERNATIVES
AND CREATIVITY

OBJECTIVES

After studying this chapter you should be able to

- identify the roots of creativity and ways to enhance your own,
- apply the mind-opening techniques of brainstorming, Osborn's list of 73 idea-spurring questions, and analogies, to identify an extensive and creative list of alternatives.

One important alternative to consider, in any analysis, is called the *do nothing* alternative. What would happen if things were kept the same as they are now? Sometimes doing nothing is the best one can do. Indeed, the organizational model (discussed in Chapter Zero) strongly suggests that change should not be undertaken lightly, given the hardship and confusion it can cause. On the other hand, a problem probably would not be subjected to analysis unless there is something wrong with the current situation. In general, the do nothing alternative should serve as a baseline; no corrective action should be undertaken unless it is expected to improve upon the current situation.

There is another important reason to include "do nothing" on the list of alternatives, marketing the recommendation. Typically, an analyst must present a proposal to a decision maker, or even more challenging, to a group who has responsibility for the decision. In this situation, the goal is often to convince the decision maker(s) that the recommended course of action is worthwhile. Demonstrating that the recommended alternative is the best one possible is difficult. However, demonstrating that an alternative will improve the current situation better than doing nothing may be relatively straightforward and enough to convince the decision maker(s) to take action.

The next step in building a list of alternatives is to identify the obvious alternatives, including the pet preferences of the various stakeholders involved. The stakeholders will probably be involved in the eventual selection, implementation, monitoring, and/or evaluation of the decision. Giving their favored options due consideration could help establish goodwill and improve any alternative's chance of successful implementation.

At this point, the list of alternatives may seem unsatisfying, offering the same worn-out, imperfect possibilities that have been considered before. Subsequent analysis is bound to indicate that one of these imperfect choices must be the best among the limited group of alternatives considered. One way out of this trap is to identify a new and creative alternative, perhaps one that nobody has ever thought of before. Conceivably, this new alternative might be better than any of the more obvious choices. This chapter discusses the nature of creativity and presents several creativity-enhancing techniques for identifying fresh alternatives.[5]

Creativity: Youth Crime and Basketball

Boys in their late teens commit more crimes than at any other age. Indeed, youth crime is a persistent problem, especially in cities where there is a high concentration of people and property. Typical methods for combating such crime include patrolling streets and curfews.

Recently, midnight basketball leagues have emerged as a creative technique for crime control. At first the connection between playing games and reducing crime was not clear. It seemed like the authorities were pandering to the youths instead of stopping their misdeeds. On the other hand, there is a connection between basketball leagues and crime reduction. Midnight basketball provides youths with an opportunity to participate in a favorite sport, at a time when many of them would otherwise be bored. Some youths become involved with crime simply to relieve this boredom. In this indirect way, midnight basketball can help reduce the problem of youth crime.

---

[5]Couger (1995) presents twenty-two creativity-enhancing techniques designed to help the analyst think about a problem more broadly. Some of the names are quite evocative of the procedures, including wishful thinking, boundary examination, interrogatories (who-what-where-when-why-how), peaceful setting, and lotus blossom (peeling back).

BLOCKS TO CREATIVITY

Take a moment to reflect on the following questions: What is creativity? Do you know any creative people? What are they like? An alternative is typically called *creative* if it has some unusual characteristic, some feature that seems unrelated to the problem.

Finding creative alternatives requires thinking about the problem while thinking in new directions, a controlled imagination. As adults, many of us lose our ability to pretend, to imagine unusual combinations. There are so many factors in our lives that mediate against creativity. Several identified by James Adams (1986) seem particularly relevant:

- NARROW THINKING: Thinking more and more about the specifics of the problem can lead to rehashing the same obvious alternatives. Sometimes the best alternative involves a marginally related or seemingly unrelated activity.

- SATURATION: In pondering the overwhelming number of concerns that an ideal solution would have to address, no alternative seems acceptable. In one sense, this problem is the opposite of narrow thinking. In this case, the analyst is thinking about too many things at once as opposed to too few things. In another sense, both narrow thinking and saturation thinking focus too much on the problem and not on new directions where novel alternatives might be found.

- INABILITY TO INCUBATE: By definition, creative ideas are those that are not obvious. Often, an analyst must contemplate a problem for an extended period of time before unusual ideas develop. Sometimes only thinking about the problem while engaging in other activities will lead to new connections. For some people, creative ideas come to them in the middle of the night when they are sleeping, or when they are driving in the car, or playing a game. Creativity can often be enhanced by engaging in activities that help one relax, reduce anxiety, let the mind roam, put one in a good mood, and perhaps even make one a little silly. Some suggestions are meditating, jogging, listening to music, going to a secluded place, or starting fresh in the morning. Which technique works best for any particular analyst is a highly individual matter.

- FEAR OF TAKING RISKS: Adults often suppress unusual ideas because they sound silly or perhaps weird and they afraid of looking dumb. These pressures can reduce an analyst's ability to ponder fresh alternatives. An ability to laugh and a willingness to be wrong can often help unleash creativity.

BRAINSTORMING

Brainstorming entails quickly writing an extensive and varied list of alternatives. (This technique can also be used to develop a broad list of objectives.) In order to keep the creative energy flowing, each idea is developed only sketchily. By focusing on quantity and variety, brainstorming helps to overcome narrow thinking and reduce the fear of looking foolish, which can impede creativity. The key to brainstorming is to separate the processes of generating ideas from the process of evaluating them. Brainstorming typically leads to an initially overwhelming number of alternatives. However, many of the ideas are usually quite similar or totally impractical. The list can often be reduced to a more manageable size with limited effort. (The process of culling the final list is discussed at the end of this chapter.)

Brainstorming can be done alone with a pen and a pad of paper. However, there is a special dynamic to holding a brainstorming session with a group. When brainstorming in a group, one person acts as facilitator, encouraging the other participants and recording ideas on a blackboard for all to view. Everyone, including the facilitator, calls out ideas as they think of them. To keep things moving, each idea is presented only superficially. The idea originator explains the idea only enough so that everyone understands it. Then the floor is reopened. Typically, brainstorming sessions are energetic and noisy.

Creative ideas can be fragile. Therefore, while brainstorming it is important to create an open, nonjudgmental, and upbeat feeling. To this end, no one should be allowed to openly judge an idea as bad. During a brainstorming session, when an idea sounds totally ridiculous and particularly unusual a useful response is "That's creative!" Using this expression as a reward encourages participants to search broadly for new and different ideas.

Quite often, one suggestion leads to another similar idea, and then another, a phenomenon known as hitch-hiking. These subsequent revisions can help a ridiculous, off-the-wall suggestion lead to a creative alternative. Thus while brainstorming, it is perfectly acceptable to suggest an idea that improves upon a preceding idea. It is not acceptable to disdain another's idea as unrealistic (or even worse, as dumb).

OSBORN'S 73 IDEA-SPURRING QUESTIONS

Osborn suggests another approach to breaking out of narrow thinking and avoiding the fear of idea generation. His list of 73 generic questions challenges the decision analyst to approach a problem from a variety of directions. To use this tool, an analyst applies each suggested transformation to a decision problem. For example, what would your problem or a potential solution look like if you turned it backwards, doing the last step first and the first step last? Depending on the problem, this suggestion might be ridiculous. In that case, had you proposed the idea you might have been embarrassed. But since it was mechanically generated from Osborn's list, everyone can laugh at the idea. On the other hand, this creative idea might lead to a viable alternative that would not otherwise have been considered.

Osborn's 73 Idea-Spurring Questions

<u>Put to other uses?</u> New ways to use as is? Other uses if modified?

<u>Adapt?</u> What else is like this? What other ideas does this suggest? Does the past offer a parallel? What could I copy? Whom could I emulate?

<u>Modify?</u> New twist? Change meaning, color, motion, sound, odor, form, shape? Other changes?

<u>Magnify?</u> What to add? More time? Greater frequency? Stronger? Higher? Longer? Thicker? Extra value? Plus ingredient? Duplicate? Multiply? Exaggerate?

<u>Minify?</u> What to subtract? Smaller? Condensed? Miniature? Lower? Shorter? Lighter? Omit? Streamline? Split up? Understate?

<u>Substitute?</u> Who else instead? What else instead? Other ingredient? Other material? Other process? Other power? Other place? Other approach? Other tone of voice?

<u>Rearrange?</u> Interchange components? Other pattern? Other layout? Other sequence? Transpose cause and effect? Change pace? Change schedule?

<u>Reverse?</u> Transpose positive and negative? How about opposites? Turn it backward? Turn it upside down? Reverse roles? Change shoes? Turn tables? Turn other cheek?

<u>Combine?</u> How about a blend, an alloy, an assortment, an ensemble? Combine units? Combine purposes? Combine appeals? Combine ideas?

Source: Adapted from Osborn (1963) with permission of Macmillan Publishing Company.

ANALOGIES

For many decision problems, the flimsy ideas generated by brainstorming or by using Osborn's list are unlikely to be practical. To identify creative alternatives that are more fully developed, an analyst can use *analogies*, comparisons with similar situations. In this way, the analyst considers adapting a fully developed solution for another problem to the current problem at hand. Finding analogies involves asking the following types of questions: What problems are similar to this one? How have they been dealt with in the past? Who else has to deal with similar problems? How do they deal with them?

The problem at hand and the analogous problem should be similar at some underlying level. On the surface, however, they may be quite different. Creative analogies are those that relate problems that appear in widely different contexts.

Many creative analogies involve comparisons with well-known situations from nature, sports, traditional industries, or nursery rhymes. These analogous situations are often easier to understand because they are physical. These types of analogous problems are called *physical systems* because the interrelationship among the situation's elements can be readily visualized, perhaps even grabbed and rolled over in one's hands. Benjamin Franklin and Abraham Lincoln were famous for their use of homespun analogies that helped everyone see complex national and international problems in everyday terms. This approach may seem woodsy and quaint, but it is still widely used today. Our language is filled with colorful analogies, such as rub the wrong way, playing with fire, brainstorming, as clever as a fox, as stubborn as a mule, as strong as an ox, like a rolling stone, like a needle in a haystack, between a rock and a hard place, on top of the world, on the right track, cast a wide net, take a step forward, score a touchdown, a home run, two points.

Searching for an analogy can help a decision analyst who is overburdened by a problem's complexity to relax and solve the problem as a whole. The following figure illustrates the process. The first step is to identify a physical system that somehow resembles the current problem. Analogies help reduce the strangeness and complexity of a problem by casting it in familiar terms. Indeed, the consequences and appropriate course of action in the analogous situations are often quite obvious. Everyone agrees that you can catch more flies with honey than vinegar, you should not to count your chickens before they hatch, you have to kiss a lot of frogs to find a prince, and an ounce of prevention is worth a pound of cure. Once such an analogy is invoked, the solution to the physical system can be creatively adapted to the current problem.

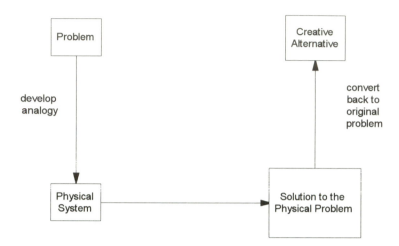

Using an Analogy to Identify a Creative Alternative

A well-suited analogy may actually identify the best solution. If the underlying structures of two problems are identical or close enough, then the solution to each must be the same. An analyst must make a judgment in determining when two problems are similar enough. Forecasting (discussed in Chapter Four) involves a similar process. Indeed, analogies can be used to provide a forecast.

Analogies: The Crack Epidemic, Part II

Bruce D. Johnson, Jeffrey Fagan, and I prepared a recommendation suggesting how New York City might cope with the widespread use of Crack cocaine prevailing in the 1990s.[6] Crack cocaine provides the user with an intense, short-lived euphoria. Its use became popular in the mid-1980s, raising concerns about protecting impressionable youths from a dangerous lifestyle, and protecting the community from violence, property crime, child abuse, and prostitution. To understand the nature of the epidemic and explain it to others, we employed numerous analogies.

Bruce D. Johnson has studied drug abuse for more than twenty years. Much of his previous research examined the Heroin Injection Epidemic, prevailing in New York City during the 1960s and early 1970s. In the 1950s heroin injection became fashionable among jazz musicians and their associates. During the 1960s, many youths revolted against conventional society and searched for alternative lifestyles. Many of these individuals experimented with hard drugs,

---

[6]Bruce D. Johnson, Andrew Golub, and Jeffrey Fagan (1995), "Careers in Crack, Drug Use, Drug Distribution and Nondrug Criminality." *Crime & Delinquency*, 41(3): 275-295.

resulting in a rapid increase in the number of heroin injectors.

In many respects the growth in use of crack cocaine during the 1980s and 1990s paralleled the growth in heroin injection prevailing in the 1960s and 1970s. Based on this similarity, we projected a similar trajectory for the Crack Epidemic as occurred with the Heroin Injection Epidemic. Today, a middle-aged core of heroin injectors who first started in the 1960s and 1970s persist in their habits. By analogy, we projected that even though crack is widely disdained in the 1990s, many of the current users in New York City will persist through the 2010s, if left unchecked.

In preparing the final report for this study, we realized that the media, politicians, and many scholars viewed the Crack Epidemic as similar to a fire blazing out of control. Indeed, scattered adjectives throughout the report already implicity made such an analogy. We decided to explicitly continue with this fire-fighting metaphor to add color and emphasis to the discussion of alternative responses. Here is a list of analogous solutions for fighting fires and responding to the Crack Epidemic:

Fire Fighting	Crack Epidemic Response
Pour water on it	Have the police crackdown on sellers and users
Let it fizzle out on its own	Wait, people will eventually become wise to the dangers of long-term use of crack
Cut a fire break	Teach children about the long-term health consequences of crack use
Remove dry timbers and other fire hazards	Address other social problems like education, employment, and moral development to reduce the conditions that lead to drug abuse

Our final suggestion was quite similar to the recommendation of many fire protection professionals. Whenever possible reduce potential fire hazards. We suggested addressing the myriad social problems leading to despair and disenfranchisement, which would reduce the rough-and-tumble material upon which the flames of social conflagration feed.

CULLING THE LIST

Creativity-enhancing exercises can yield a profusion of alternatives. Having too many alternatives can lead to a very lengthy analysis. On the other hand, having too few alternatives can lead to the selection of an inferior alternative. A large list of alternatives should be reduced in order to ease subsequent analysis, yet without unnecessarily reducing the range of alternatives. The final list should include the one alternative of each "type" that appears to be most promising.

❐ SUMMARY

The quality of an analyst's eventual recommendation is limited by the range of alternatives considered. The best solution will not be chosen unless it is included in the analysis. However, one cannot tell which is the best solution prior to analysis. In this regard, it is advantageous to identify a wide range of alternatives.

Identifying some of the more unique and potentially outstanding solutions requires creativity. An analyst's creativity is often hampered by thinking too narrowly, becoming overwhelmed with a problem's complexity, not taking enough time to ponder possible alternatives, and a fear of looking foolish. Several creativity-enhancing techniques can help overcome these barriers, including brainstorming, Osborn's 73 Idea-Spurring Questions, and making analogies. These techniques can help an analyst identify a large and varied list of alternatives. Prior to further analysis, the list of alternatives for consideration should be narrowed to a manageable size. This final list should encompass a range of promising alternatives in addition to the do-nothing alternative and those alternatives most favored by various stakeholders.

❐ EXERCISES

1. Create physical analogies to the following problems and identify a solution suggested by the analogy.

    a. Employee theft.
    b. Traffic jams.
    c. Teenage pregnancy.
    d. Providing service in a busy hospital emergency room.
    e. Marketing a new line of prepared, frozen dinners.
    f. Employees with preschool-aged children's need for child care.
    g. Unemployment.
    h. Motivating members of the telemarketing staff.

❐ FOR YOUR PROJECT

1. Allot yourself thirty minutes in a quiet room to brainstorm on alternative solutions to your problem. Consider engaging in a creativity-enhancing activity, such as jogging or meditating prior, to your session. Make sure you spend at least half-an-hour brainstorming to allow ideas to incubate.

2. Get together with at least two colleagues and lead a group brainstorming session. Compare the results of this session to the one you did by yourself.

3. Create an analogy between your problem and a physical system. Based on your analogy, identify at least one possible solution.

4. Combine all of your lists to create one comprehensive list of possible alternatives. Reduce this list to a reasonable number of the most promising yet varied candidates for further consideration.

❒ FOR ADDITIONAL INFORMATION ON

Creativity:

Adams, James L. 1986. *Conceptual Blockbusting: A Guide to Better Ideas,* 2nd ed.. Reading, MA: Addison-Wesley.

Couger, J. Daniel. 1995. *Creative Problem Solving and Opportunity Finding.* Danvers, MA: Boyd & Fraser, a division of International Thomson.

Davis, Gary. 1986. *Creativity Is Forever*, 2nd ed.. Dubuque, IA: Kendall/Hunt.

Dunn, William N. 1994. *Public Policy Analysis: An Introduction*, 2nd ed. Englewood Cliffs, NJ: Prentice Hall.

Osborn, A. F. 1963. *Applied Imagination*, 3rd ed. New York: Scribner's.

Chapter Four
FORECASTING AND
SUBJECTIVE ASSESSMENT

OBJECTIVES
After studying this chapter you should be able to

- use probability in two different ways: first, as a way of expressing the long-term frequency with which a repeated event occurs; second, as a method for quantifying uncertainty over whether an event will occur,

- elicit a decision maker's subjective assessment of the probability an event will occur,

- develop a decomposition of events or fault tree to describe the series of dependent events that could lead to a larger event of interest,

- quantitatively express your assessment of a forecast's accuracy.

A *forecast* is a vision that identifies what the future will be like or several possible future outcomes that might prevail. The previous steps of the rational model have fully specified the structure of the decision problem, but not the numbers to be used in the analysis. Foreaasting involves identifying the numbers that characterize what the future might be like, including the probabilities associated with uncertain events and any operational measures. Chapter Five examines the last group of numbers, values. As indicated in Chapter Two, operational measures specify what the future might be like and values specify how the decision maker feels about them.

This chapter describes several different approaches and techniques for obtaining a forecast. A forecast specifies an analyst's understanding of the dynamics of a situation and is, therefore, the core of any decision analysis. An essential problem is that the future cannot always be known with certainty. Forecasts are not facts. As a result, forecasts for the same decision problem often vary across individuals. The choice as to which forecast to use is often up to an analyst's subjective judgment.

Some forecasts are more accurate than others. Individuals who have extensive knowledge of a subject, called *experts*, can often provide more accurate, more plausible forecasts than others. In this regard, the validity of any recommendation depends on the quality of the expert providing the forecast. Consequently, you should choose to make recommendations in areas where you have much expertise. If you are called upon to make a recommendation in an area with which you are less familiar, you might consider hiring an expert to help supply you with a forecast. Alternatively, you could develop your own expertise by reading the literature, taking courses, and interviewing experts.

MODELS

A *model* is a simplified representation of the key elements of reality and their interaction. Decision analysts use models to provide a foundation for their forecasts. The real world is rather complicated. To develop a clear vision of the consequences of various actions, a forecaster often decides what facts and relationships are essential and disregards everything else. The diagram below presents the modeling process (Brewer and DeLeon, 1995, p. 151).

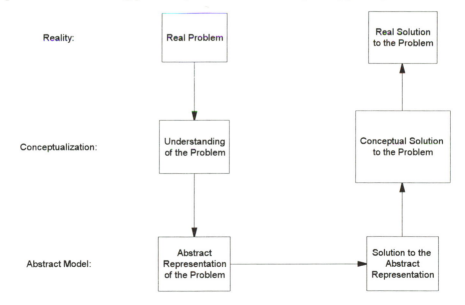

The figure illustrates how decision analysis starts with a real problem occurring in the real world. The world is filled with complexity and is often difficult to understand completely. The analyst's comprehension of the problem is called his or her *conceptual understanding*. This perception of the problem identifies what facts are important and how they are interrelated. From this conceptual understanding, the analyst might develop an *abstract model* that specifies with great precision the mathematics of what would happen if various courses of action were pursued. This would form the basis of any forecast. Such a model can indicate, in theory, which alternative should lead to the best possible outcome. Based on this best theoretical alternative, an analyst could develop a plan of action. Once implemented, such an action, theoretically, should help lead to a real solution to the real problem.

The primary problem with the use of models is that in each transition to a deeper level–from reality to concept, and from concept to abstract model–information is lost. To the extent that the analyst's understanding of the problem is incomplete, extensive information is lost between the real problem and its conceptualization.

Information is typically lost in the process of developing a mathematical model. It is useful to include as much detail in the model as possible so that it captures the complexity of the analyst's conceptual understanding of the problem. However, complicated models become hard to solve. Hence, forecasters often try to identify the simplest models possible that will lend insight into the problem at hand. The gap between the complexity of the real world and the simplicity of the abstract models that forecasters often use leads to the following credo of humility for mathematical modeling: *All models are wrong; some models are useful.*

As an alternative to developing a mathematical model, an analyst can go directly from a conceptual understanding of the problem to a conceptual solution. This typically involves writing scenarios describing what would happen were each of the various alternatives implemented. This approach has the advantage of eliminating the potential information loss inherent in delving into an abstract model.

Abstract Models

There are a variety of mathematical models that can be applied to problems in the business, government and personal domains. A detailed discussion of each of them is beyond the scope of this book. Many of the more versatile models are covered in courses on forecasting, management science, and operations research. The following brief typology illustrates the range and variety of these models.

- DETERMINISTIC MODELS: These models are particularly useful for representing the complex interaction between a large number of elements. Widely used deterministic models include linear programming, nonlinear programming, differential equations, and combinatorics.

- PROBABILITY MODELS: Unlike deterministic models, probability models explicitly incorporate uncertainty. Typically, these models can incorporate fewer elements than their deterministic counterparts, before they become too complicated to solve. Widely used probability models include queuing theory, game theory, linear regression, logistic regression, time series analysis, and path analysis.

- SIMULATION MODELS: The various classes of deterministic and probabilistic models place strong restrictions on the structure of the problem.   This limited complexity typically ensures that some widely-available solution procedure can be used to determine the best alternative.   Simulation models can simultaneously incorporate complex interactions among elements and probability.   However, this additional complexity comes with a price.   The process of verifying the reasonableness of a complicated simulation model is more involved than for basic deterministic and probabilistic models.

- DISCIPLINE SPECIFIC MODELS: The evolution of many sciences has been guided by the need for help with specific types of decision making. The literature in these fields typically identifies a variety of specific formulations that have been found useful over time. Economists often rely upon models of supply and demand.   Other fields, such as operations management, organization theory, psychology, sociology, ecology, meteorology, and medicine, have their own histories of mathematical modeling.

Conceptual Models

A decision analyst may choose not to develop a formal mathematical model for a wide variety of reasons: Abstract models may be overly simplistic, modeling can take too long, or the analyst already understands the problem well enough. In lieu of a mathematical model, an analyst can work directly from a conceptual understanding of a problem to forecast the impact of various alternative actions.

This approach is often criticized as being openly subjective because it relies heavily on the decision analyst's conceptual vision, which may be biased. On the other hand, the choice of which mathematical model to use is also subjective and dependent on expert judgment. Hence, using mathematics does not in and of itself guarantee an objective forecast. Mathematical models are based on assumptions about how the real world operates—assumptions that can be wrong. However, because of their rigorous structure, a mathematical model forces an analyst to explicitly identify the central assumptions behind an analysis. Once identified, these assumptions can be criticized, leading to potential modifications of the model. Conceptual models are less explicit and, consequently, can be more difficult to modify.

Conceptual forecasts are typically based on analogies. Even though each decision problem is unique, one might contend that no problem is completely new. There is usually someone somewhere who has encountered a similar problem. That experience can suggest what would happen to the current situation were various alternatives implemented. Some problems are encountered so frequently, that informal theories develop to summarize the dynamics of the situation. Such analogies are more or less compelling to the extent that the current situation resembles the previous situation.

Often, different theories or analogies lead to conflicting forecasts. Such situations can serve to remind a decision analyst that the future is uncertain. To reconcile such conflicts in practice, an analyst might add an uncertain event to the representation of the decision problem and identify the result suggested by each competing theory as a possible outcome. The probability of each outcome can represent the relative degree to which the current situation resembles situations in which each theory tends to hold.

Conceptual Models: Action Fragrance, Part II

The Ectron Fragrance Corporation is considering producing a new fragrance named Action, designed for youthful, athletic women. These women traditionally do not tend to buy much fragrance. Ectron is wondering whether this is because none of the current products appeal to them or because these women actually dislike the use of perfume. They created the following three possible scenarios to indicate their uncertainty:

High Sales: Active women will be thrilled by a new perfume designed for their lifestyle, leading to excellent sales.

Low Sales: Active women dislike fragrance, even ones designed especially for them. These women will avoid use of Action as much as they avoid use of other perfumes, leading to poor sales.

Medium Sales: Some active women will be intrigued by a special scent for them, and others will not be. Overall, the new product will fill a niche and sales will be moderate.

Since these women traditionally do not use fragrance, the low-sales scenario seemed most compelling; the high-sales scenario seemed like a long-shot. The medium-sales scenario also appeared quite compelling since the product is specially designed for these women. Ectron attached the following probabilities to the possible outcomes: Pr[High Sales] = 10%, Pr[Medium Sales] = 40% Pr[Low Sales] = 50%.

FORECASTING PROBABILITIES

Irrespective of whether one uses a conceptual or an abstract model to develop a forecast, it is necessary to obtain probabilities associated with uncertain events. The remainder of this chapter focuses on methods to obtain these inputs, but first the chapter discusses how decision analysts think about the use of probability, in the abstract.

Three Uses of Probability

Probability can be used in three different ways: to express the long-term frequency of a recurring chance event, to quantify a lack of knowledge about a past event, and to express the likelihood that a unique future event will occur. The first use, expressing probability as a long-term frequency, is widely accepted and is known as the *classical* or *frequentist* use of probability. The latter two uses rely on an individual's personal assessment and are, therefore, referred to as the *subjective* or *Bayesian* use of probability.

Bayesian probability is somewhat controversial because of its use of subjectivity.   Clearly, probabilities established through experience with a frequently recurring event have a stronger foundation than an expert's "best guess." However, for practical decision making, the subjective view of probability can prove quite useful. As a result, there is much research into Bayesian methods of probability and statistics and acceptance of these methods is growing rapidly. This book employs all three uses of probability because it increases a decision maker's ability to include all types of information in a decision analysis.

The nature of the three uses of probability can be illustrated with variations on a familiar problem; guessing the outcome of a coin flip. These simple exercises illustrate their fundamental differences and the basis for controversy regarding the subjective use of probability.

A typical coin is virtually symmetric. Consequently, if you flip it in the air and let it fall to the ground, it is just as likely to land heads up as opposed to tails up. Thus, the probability of heads is about 50%, as is the probability of tails. Another way of thinking of this is that if you flipped a coin 100 times, it would probably come up heads about 50 times. In this sense, the long-term frequency of heads is 50 out of 100 or 50%.

Long-Term Frequency, Coin-Flip Experiment
Take a coin out of your wallet, purse, or wherever you keep spare change. You are going to flip it into the air and let it fall to the ground. What is the probability that it will come up heads?

This is a fairly noncontroversial question. Most people have flipped a coin on many occasions and have found that heads appears about every other time. If the coin looks like a fair coin, it seems reasonable to extrapolate that there's a 50% chance of heads on a future trial of the coin-flipping experiment.

Uncertainty About the Past, Coin-Flip Experiment
Flip your coin into the air, catch it in your hand, and slap it on top of your other hand. Be sure not to look at it yet. What is the probability that it came up heads?

This experiment seems like the first except with a subtle twist–the event already occurred. This often takes the excitement out of the experiment. In a similar sense, many people will not watch a sporting event televised after the fact, even if they have not yet heard the final scores.

One could argue that the probability of heads in the second experiment is still 50%. Before the coin was flipped it had a 50% probability of heads. Knowing that the coin was flipped did not provide any new information about whether this trial was heads or tails. Thus, after the coin was flipped, the probability remains at 50%. This is the Bayesian viewpoint. In this case, the probability identifies your ignorance about the outcome. Someone else who looked at the coin can know the outcome with certainty, but you don't.

On the other hand, did you find this question troubling? A staunch frequentist would argue that this is a misuse of probability. The coin landed either heads or tails and thus there is either a 100% chance of heads if it is heads, and a 0% chance of heads if it is tails. You just don't know which outcome occurred.

Uncertainty About the Past: Mr. Gomez's Tumor

Mr. Gomez went to Dr. Vandana Gupta to see about a new mole that had appeared on his neck. Dr. Gupta assured Mr. Gomez that developing a mole is not uncommon as people age, although sometimes these moles are the result of a cancerous growth. Mr. Gomez asked what the probability was that his mole was cancerous. Dr. Gupta responded by saying, "Your mole either is or is not cancerous. In my experience, about 5% of cases like yours turn out to have been cancerous. I could take a sample and perform a biopsy and then you'd know for sure."

The question of whether to perform additional tests is a common concern facing medical practice today. Prudent care suggests performing tests to be able to diagnose a patient's ailment with the greatest certainty. On the other hand, testing both inconveniences the patient and costs money. These concerns suggest that testing be kept to a minimum.

Mr. Gomez's decision can be represented by the following decision tree. The subjective assessment of the probability that Mr. Gomez's tumor is cancerous is essential to solving this decision problem, along with an understanding of the tradeoff between the various objectives.

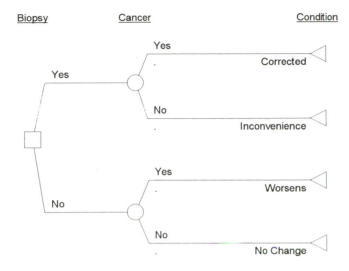

Uncertainty About a Unique Future Event, Coin-Flip Experiment
Choose an odd-shaped, everyday item with one relatively flat and one not-so-flat side, such as a hat, a spatula, or a toy truck. You are going to flip it into the air and have it land on the floor. What is the probability that it lands right-side up?

Establishing a probability in this case is tough. You probably do not have much experience flipping such an item, and so you don't have a basis for establishing a long-term frequency. A staunch frequentist would say that you cannot provide such a probability, unless you performed enough preliminary trials to establish a long-term frequency. A Bayesian would say that you can provide a probability by analogizing and reasoning. Of course, the quality of your analysis depends on the validity of your assumptions.

In the case of flipping an odd-shaped item, one's reasoning might proceed as possible: Fifty percent seems like the highest probability possible for any object that is not designed to bounce and find its correct orientation. When tossed indiscriminately, most items will usually land in some awkward orientation, more often than not. Look at the object you chose, and get a sense of how irregularly the object is shaped. A fairly robust item should have a probability of landing right-side up close to 50%. A more oddly-shaped item may have a probability close to zero. Since this assessment is subjective, your estimate may vary from what others would suggest. Of course, some analysts' subjective assessment will be more accurate than others.

The best solution to many important decision problems depends on an assessment of the probability of a unique future event. The following questions suggest some unique uncertain events that affect important decisions:

- Will Americans' enthusiasm for inline skating continue?
- Could Ron be financially successful as a private consultant?
- Can Microsoft continue to be an innovator and market leader?
- Would Bosnian military forces abide by a peace treaty?

Each of these events is so unique that it is not feasible to try the experiment over and over. However, important decisions require an assessment of the probability of each. For decision problems involving these and similar unique uncertain events occurring in the future, it is practical to use subjective probabilities.

The Direct Method for Eliciting Probabilities

This chapter presents three approaches for eliciting the probability associated with an uncertain event from an expert: the direct method, the betting method, and the comparison lottery method. The direct method proceeds as straightforwardly as it sounds. Simply ask an expert what he or she thinks is the probability of an event. Experts who are used to providing quantitative forecasts, such as meteorologists, are typically prepared to provide such precise quantitative responses. Such expertise may be informed by a study of prior similar situations, a mathematical model, a poll, a pilot study, or a combination of these tempered by personal judgment. Other experts may not be used to expressing themselves so abstractly. The betting and comparison lottery methods are designed to help such experts visualize probabilities in more familiar contexts.

The Betting Method for Eliciting Probabilities

Many people are used to dealing with probabilities through the pastime of gambling, especially when it comes to sports. Many avid sports fans are also avid gamblers and are always ready to test their sports knowledge through betting. These gamblers can typically tell you which team they feel is more likely to win. Moreover, such gamblers will often provide the precise odds for which they would be willing to bet on a game. These odds indicate the gambler's perception of each team's relative likelihood of winning. Indeed, odds are just another way of expressing a probability. Every statement about odds corresponds to a statement about probability. For example, a team with two-to-one odds in its favor is twice as likely to win as lose. This corresponds to a 66⅔% chance of winning and a 33⅓% chance of losing.

The Betting Method: The Giants-Eagles Football Game

Uncertainty about the future lends much excitement to watching sporting events. Sports fans often enjoy discussing their sense of uncertainty and actually talk about an individual or team's likelihood of winning.   Quite often, this uncertainty is expressed as the odds of winning. For example, the odds that the New York Giants will beat the Philadelphia Eagles in a football game could be two-to-one in their favor. This means that the Giants are two times more likely to win the game than are the Eagles.

Moreover, some sports fans enjoy participating in the uncertainty associated with a game through gambling. A simple sports bet might involve each gambler providing ten dollars and choosing which side will win the game. Whichever gambler's team wins the game takes the entire twenty dollars. Partisan feelings aside, which team would you choose in the New York-Philadelphia game described above? Given the odds, the smart money would be on the Giants. In fact, in this situation you might have great difficulty finding anyone to take the Eagles' side of this gamble.

Sports gamblers have various methods for making the bet more fair. One approach involves setting the payoffs according to the odds. Each gambler provides a gambling stake in proportion to the odds of winning. In this case, the gambler betting on the Eagles would put up $10, and the gambler betting on the Giants would put up $20. The gambler whose team wins collects the other gambler's bet.

This second betting system can be considered fair. The gambler betting on the Giants has twice as much of a chance of winning, but can win only half as much as the gambler betting on the Eagles ($10 winning on a $20 bet). The gambler betting on the Eagles has half the chance of winning, but can collect double ($20 on a $10 bet). In this manner, the expected winnings associated with each side of the gamble are the same, zero, as indicated in the decision tree below.

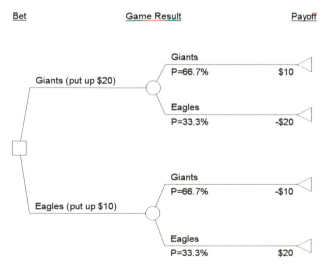

| Bet | Game Result | Payoff |

Giants
P=66.7% $10

Giants (put up $20)

Eagles
P=33.3%   -$20

Eagles (put up $10)

Giants
P=66.7%   -$10

Eagles
P=33.3% $20

The betting method involves eliciting an individual's odds for an event as a hypothetical gamble and then converting those odds into a probability. Some people might have difficulty identifying their odds. For these experts, the technique of *bracketing*, or slowly narrowing in on the expert's odds, can be useful. This procedure entails asking easy questions about the odds and building up to a more-accurate assessment. Each assessment is based on the following gamble:

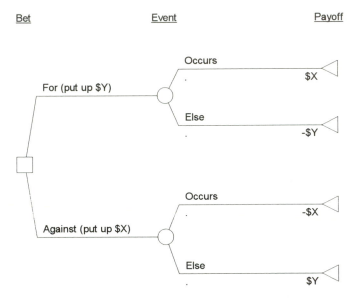

The even-money gamble provides a convenient starting point. The expert is asked to choose a preferred side of the gamble, given that the payoff for correctly predicting the occurrence of the event is the same as for correctly predicting its nonoccurrence. In this case, both X and Y might be equal to one dollar. The expert could choose to bet on the occurrence of the event. If it occurs, the expert would receive $1. If it does not occur, the expert loses $1. Alternatively, the expert could choose the converse gamble, in which case the payoffs are reversed.

The odds in this gamble are expressed as Y-to-X in favor of the event, which in this case is one-to-one. One-to-one corresponds to a 50% probability that the event occurs. The goal of the analysis is to find the odds for which the expert perceives that the bet is fair. The odds at which an expert perceives the expected payoffs for and against gambling on an event are equal are called the expert's *indifference odds*. When presented with a gamble based on the indifference odds, the expert will be indifferent between betting for or against the occurrence of the event because the expected payoff for each event will be zero.

Let's assume that the expert chose to bet for the event. Such a choice would indicate that the expert perceives the event is more likely to occur than not or that the odds for the event are greater than one-to-one. A set of odds that are definitely below the expert's indifference odds are called a *lower bound*.

The next step is to establish a set of odds for which the expert would definitely bet against the occurrence of the event, which is called an *upper bound*. This can be accomplished by offering the expert odds that dramatically favor betting against the occurrence of the event, such as ten to one. In this scenario, $X = \$1$ and $Y = \$10$. Faced with this paltry yield for correctly predicting that the event would occur, the expert might switch to betting against the event. Such a bet would indicate that the expert perceives that the odds for the event are less than ten to one. If the expert chooses to bet for the event, it indicates that the odds in the revised gamble also provide a lower bound on the indifference odds. In this case, the analyst might try a much higher set of odds, perhaps one hundred or one thousand to one.

Once the analyst knows a lower and upper bound, the expert's perceived indifference odds are said to be *bracketed*; they must be between these two bounds. As described above, these bounds might be fairly wide, such as between one to one and ten to one. The process at this point is to hone in on the expert's indifference odds. One might try to narrow the bounds as quickly as possible and choose a next set of odds such as five to one. In proceeding quickly, however, there is a risk of asking a tough question that the expert will have great difficulty answering, at least at this time. Therefore, it is often best to narrow the bounds slowly. For example, if it is known that the expert would bet against the event if the odds were ten to one, the analyst might try asking about odds of eight to one. Eight to one is not that much different from ten to one, and the expert might still bet against the event for these odds.

The narrowing procedure of finding successively higher lower bounds and successively lower upper bounds continues until the difference between the two converge on the same value, the expert's indifference odds. The expert would bet against the occurrence of the event for any odds above that value and for the occurrence of the event below that value.

At this point, the expert's subjective assessment of the event's probability can be deduced. The fact that the expert perceives the expected payoffs associated with betting for and against the events implies the following:

$$EMV[\text{betting for event}] = EMV[\text{betting against event}]$$

$$X \times P \ + \ -Y \times (1 - P) \ = \ -X \times P \ + \ Y \times (1 - P)$$

Where,
$P = Pr[\text{event}]$

The formula for identifying an expert's subjective probability from indifference odds can be straightforwardly derived as follows:

$$\rightarrow \quad 2 \times X \times P = 2 \times Y \times (1-P)$$

$$X \times P = Y \times (1-P)$$

$$X \times P = Y - Y \times P$$

$$X \times P + Y \times P = Y$$

$$P \times (X + Y) = Y$$

$$\rightarrow \quad P = \frac{Y}{X + Y}$$

The steps of the betting method are summarized as follows:

Steps to the Betting Method for Eliciting the Probability of an Event
1. DETERMINE INDIFFERENCE ODDS: Follow these steps to identify an expert's indifference odds:

    a. SET UP THE GAMBLE: Identify the gamble in which the expert can choose to bet for or against the event's occurrence as illustrated in the following decision tree:

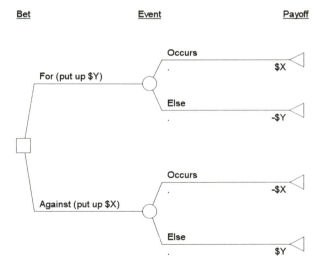

    b. NARROW IN ON THE INDIFFERENCE ODDS: Successively vary the payoff values, X and Y, to narrow in on the point at which the expert switches from betting for to betting against occurrence of the event. Maintain a table of the expert's preferred bet for each set of payoffs ordered according to the indifference odds, the ratio $Y \div X$:

		Indifference	Preferred
X	Y	Odds (Y ÷ X)	Gamble
			against

for

    c. IDENTIFY THE INDIFFERENCE ODDS: Identify the intermediate odds Y to X for which the expert is just as willing to bet for as against occurrence of the event.

2. CONVERT INDIFFERENCE ODDS INTO A PROBABILITY: Use the following formula to convert the expert's betting preference into a probability.

$$P = \frac{Y}{X+Y}$$

The Betting Method: The Election
The future of democratic government depends on the individuals elected to serve. Each candidate typically has an agenda for the future. Whether a candidate has the opportunity to implement his or her agenda depends on the outcome of the vote. The following discussion between a candidate and a campaign manager illustrates the process of estimating the probability of an uncertain event, in this case the event that the candidate wins the election.

Candidate: So how am I doing? Will I win the election? How are my chances?

Manager: I just ran a poll, and it shows that you are ahead. If the vote were held today, you would win with 58% of the vote.

Candidate: That's great news. Does that mean that I'm going to win, or that I have a 58% chance of winning?

Manager: No, neither; I can't tell you what your chances are, because people can change their vote. Many things can happen between now and November.

Candidate: I see. However, I need to know my chances in order to make some important decisions. Let's try a technique that I know from decision analysis. Tell me, you're a hockey fan aren't you? You'd probably be willing to give me odds on whether the Pittsburgh Penguins will win the Stanley Cup this year.

Manager: Hey, that's interesting! I gamble on sports all the time.

Candidate: Let's combine your gambling talents with your expert knowledge
about elections, my platform, and the electorate to determine a
probability estimate for my winning this election. Look at the
following gamble. Would you bet a thousand dollars on my
election, of course, only hypothetically?

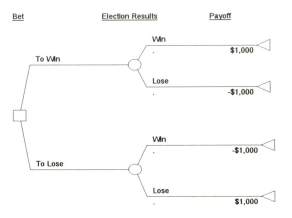

Manager: No question. I would definitely bet on your election.

Candidate: Great; now consider the following gamble paying ten to one
odds:

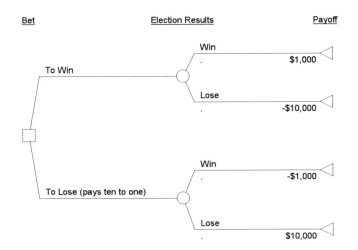

Manager: Hey boss, I don't want to appear disloyal and bet against you!

Candidate: I really appreciate that, but put on your gambling hat for this exercise. Think about this as purely a test of your gambling ability and not of your loyalty to me! Besides, this is only hypothetical.

Manager: Well if that's the way you feel, then at those odds I would bet against you.

Candidate: Now we're getting somewhere, let me make a table of our findings so far.

X	Y	Indifference Odds (Y ÷ X)	Preferred Gamble
$1,000	$10,000	10:1	against
$1,000	$1,000	1:1	for

Let's consider another gamble. Which bet would you take this time?

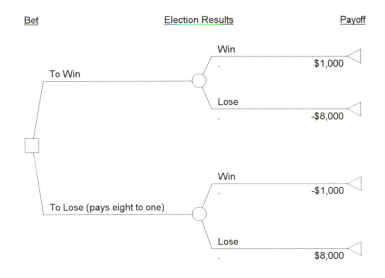

Manager: I would still bet against you.

Candidate: How about for $6,000?

Manager: Against you.

Candidate: How about $4,000?

Manager: Now that's getting tough!

Candidate: Ok, let's try it the other way. How about for $2,000?

Manager: Then, I would definitely bet for you.

Candidate: And for $3,000?

Manager: That's getting tough, again!

Candidate: Let's recap now. Here's your betting record:

X	Y	Indifference Odds (Y ÷ X)	Preferred Gamble
$1,000	$10,000	10:1	against
$1,000	$8,000	8:1	against
$1,000	$6,000	6:1	against
$1,000	$2,000	2:1	for
$1,000	$1,000	1:1	for

Candidate: So we know that you would bet against me if the payoff were at least $6,000, and for me if the payoff is no higher than $2,000. The goal of this exercise is to find the dollar amount at which you would find each bet equally desirable. It must be somewhere between $2,000 and $6,000.

Manager: I'd say that point would be at about $3,500.

Candidate: OK, let me confirm that. You would be indifferent between the two alternatives in the following gambling problem.

This implies that you would set the odds at 3.5 to 1 in favor of my winning the election.

Manager: Hey, that sounds reasonable.

Candidate: Let me do a little arithmetic: $3.5 \div (3.5 + 1.0) = 3.5 \div 4.5 = .78$ or 78%. So, this exercise suggests you would give me a 78% chance of winning the election.

The Comparison Lottery Method for Eliciting Probabilities

The comparison lottery method presents the forecaster with a choice between participating in either of two gambles: betting on the uncertain event, or betting on a reference lottery with a known probability of winning. This reference lottery can be visualized as a partially-shaded wheel of fortune, just like one would view at the midway of a county fair. For this game, the wheel is spun and a pointer that is permanently affixed to the wheel's housing indicates one spot along the wheel's perimeter. If that point is within the shaded region, the gambler wins. This graphical orientation can help some forecasters conceive of probability as visual risk. The following diagram illustrates the central decision confronting the forecaster:

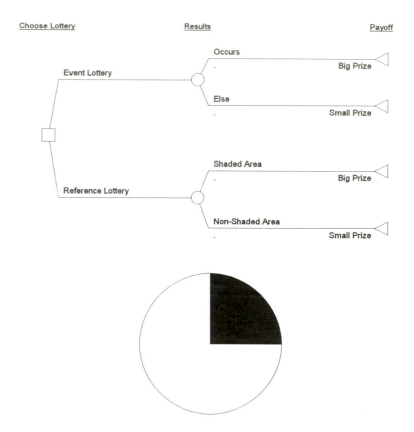

The decision problem above presents the expert with a choice between betting on the event of interest or on a reference lottery. Depending on which lottery is chosen, the expert could possibly win a big prize if either the event occurs or the pointer lands in the shaded region. Otherwise, the expert receives a small prize. The nature of the prizes does not really matter, as long as the big prize is much more desirable than the little prize, for example, a car as opposed to a pen. The expert will be motivated to choose the lottery carefully in order to win the big prize.

The goal of the comparison lottery approach is to determine a probability, P, for which the forecaster is indifferent between betting on the event or spinning the wheel of fortune. By implication, the forecaster's subjective estimate of the event's probability must be P. As with the betting method, the search for this value, P, can proceed expediently for those who are comfortable with the method or otherwise more slowly.

Comparison Lottery: Action Women Adventure Doll

Typically at Christmas time, one children's toy becomes exceedingly popular. If there is enough stock in the warehouse, a company can sell tens of millions of the season's most popular toy. However, if there is not enough of the product, parents buy other, more traditional toys. This year, Toyco thinks they have a hit with their new Action Woman Adventure Doll. They could manufacture 20 million units and hope they sell or manufacture a more modest 2 million units that will almost certainly sell. Lateacha, from marketing, has extensive experience with new product sales that includes a substantial understanding of the all-important Christmas sales. She is currently training Maxwell, who is responsible for the Action Women Adventure Doll marketing plan. The following dialogue shows how they developed a forecast for the probability that the doll will be a super hit.

Maxwell: Help! Senior management has asked me to provide them with my estimate of the probability that the Action Women Adventure Doll will be this year's big Christmas toy. I know my doll, especially after the excellent response to the test marketing. I also know how intense and fickle Christmas sales can be. How do I put it all together to give them a single number?

Lateacha: Whoever told you that marketing would be easy? Here's what I do. I study my product and my competitors in order to obtain insight into how the market is taking shape, just like you've already done. Then I go out for a good lunch. I usually order something that puts me in a good frame of mind, but also won't make me feel too full. For me that's Chinese food. All right, then I come back to the office relaxed and ready to take the plunge. I log into DPL, bring up the View Wheel option for entering the probability of an uncertain event, and prepare to do a comparison lottery. Are you game?

Maxwell: I'll try anything.

Lateacha: I find that each new product is so different, especially ones like Action Woman Adventure Doll, that I have to avoid thinking too logically and tap into my expert intuition. It's the systematic use of such a well-developed instinct that makes for a good marketing executive.

The comparison lottery centers around the following decision problem. Would you prefer to gamble on your new product making the big Christmas sales, or would you prefer to spin this wheel of fortune? If you win, I'll buy you that built-in swimming pool you've been wanting for years. If you lose, I'll take you out for Chinese food for lunch tomorrow.

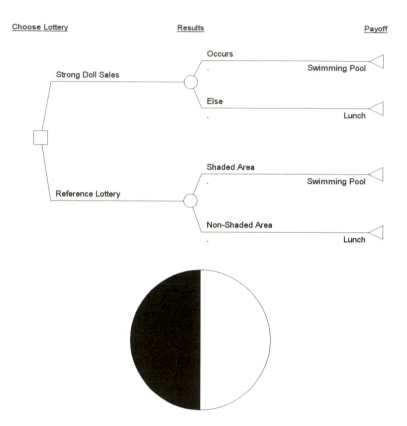

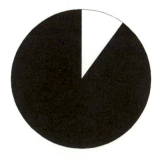

Maxwell: Hey that's neat! I know what I would do here. I would definitely bet on my doll. Test market reports seem to indicate real potential. Fifty percent is like a coin flip, and I know this doll has real potential.

Lateacha: All right then. How about if we change the reference lottery to 90%?

Maxwell: That's easy, too.   As much as I believe in Action Women Adventure Doll's potential, I don't believe anything is such a shoo-in for the big Christmas sales. I would have to go for the reference lottery.

Lateacha: How about 80%?

Maxwell: Spin the wheel.

Lateacha: How about 70%?

Maxwell: That's getting tough.

Lateacha: OK, let's recap. We have determined that your best estimate is somewhere between 50% and 80%.

Maxwell: I guess we have! That's really narrowed things down.

Lateacha: Back to the comparison lottery. How about 60%?

Maxwell: I'd go with the doll.

Lateacha: 65%?

Maxwell: The doll.

Lateacha: Good; we now know that the probability lies between 65% and 80%. Let me show you how each of those looks on the wheel of fortune.

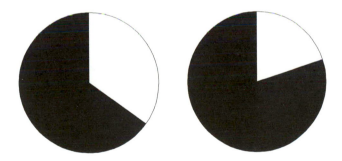

You know it has to be between 65% and 80%.

Maxwell: This looks about right.

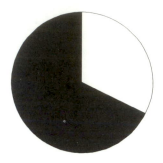

Lateacha: There's your answer.   Go tell senior management that your
             estimate for the probability that the doll is a big success is 68%.

Maxwell: I like that! Thanks for your help.

Decomposition

Sometimes it is difficult to attach a probability to an event because of its
relationship to other events.   The occurrence of an event might be heavily
influenced by the occurrence of another uncertain event. In other situations, the
occurrence of an event might be dependent on the occurrence of any one of a
number of possible uncertain events, the occurrence of a sequence of other
uncertain events, or any of various sequences of uncertain events. Often when
pressed for a probability, an expert will respond, "Well, that depends . . ." which
directly indicates the nature of the dependency.

It is often useful to create a diagram known as a *fault tree* to describe the
sequence(s) of uncertain events that affect the probability that the event of interest
occurs. These relationships can be represented in an influence diagram. Unlike
the influence diagrams used for representing decision problems, fault trees include
only uncertain events; neither decisions nor objectives are included. The figure
below presents a fault tree in which the uncertain event of interest, event A, is
dependent upon the outcome of another uncertain event, event B.

Every influence diagram has a corresponding decision tree representation.   In
fact, fault trees are called trees because historically they have usually been
presented as trees. The following fault tree corresponds to the previous influence
diagram.

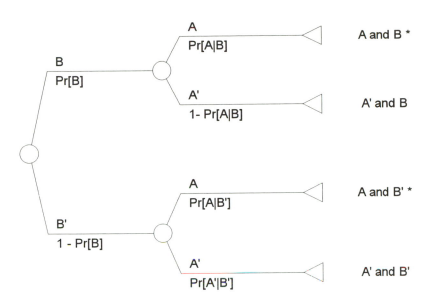

* Situations in which A occurs

The figure above explicitly identifies the conditions under which event A might occur: either subsequent to the occurrence of event B, or after non-occurrence of event B.

In order to determine the probability of event A, Pr[A], the probabilities along each of the branches in the figure above must be specified. These probabilities include the probability of the conditioning event, Pr[B], and two conditional probabilities, the probability of event A if event B occurred, Pr[A|B], and the probability of event A if event B does not occur, Pr[A|B']. In practice, conditioning events can help create the context in which an event occurs. As a result, it is often much easier to assess Pr[A|B] than Pr[A] for a well-chosen conditioning event. The probability of event A can be determined in this case using the formula for total probability (Appendix C provides a derivation of this formula and of other probabilistic relationships often useful in analyzing decision problems):

$$Pr[A] = Pr[A|B] \times Pr[B] + Pr[A|B'] \times Pr[A|B']$$

Decomposition: Governmental Transition in Cuba
What is the probability that Cuba will change to a democratic form of government next year? The likelihood of such an occurrence seemed quite remote years ago. However, the collapse of the Soviet Union clearly showed that communist governments can dissolve.

When discussing the future of Cuba, everything seems to be tied to Fidel Castro, a charismatic and powerful leader who has ruled the country since 1959.

He is getting older. Eventually, he will have to leave his position, perhaps as the result of deteriorating health. In this way, the probability of democratic reforms in Cuba depends on Castro's health, as illustrated below:

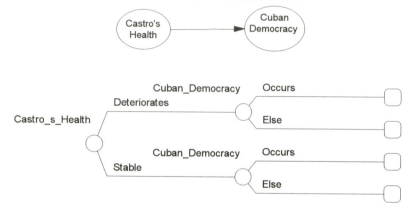

Given Castro's advancing age and the nature of human mortality, one might assess the probability of his health taking a substantial turn for the worse to be 20%. If his health deteriorates, then a governmental transition will have to take place. The probability that a successor will emerge who wishes to maintain the country as it is and has the power to do so seems somewhat remote. Thus, democratic reforms under these circumstances might have a 60% chance of occurrence. Given Castro's good health, the chance that he should have a change of heart and consider instituting a democratic government is remote, but not unthinkable. Perhaps there is a 5% chance.

The total probability of democratic reform in Cuba can be calculated as follows:

$$\Pr[D] = \Pr[D|C] \times \Pr[C] + \Pr[D|C'] \times (1 - \Pr[C])$$

Where,
D = Democratic reform in Cuba
C = Castro's health deteriorates

$$\Pr[D] = .60 \times .20 + .05 \times .80 = .16$$

This suggests that there is a 16% total chance of democratic reforms in Cuba next year.

DPL can perform calculations of total probability by attaching an objective node to the end of the fault tree as follows:

Next, the value of the new objective node is specified to equal one if democracy prevails, and zero otherwise. Solving the decision problem in DPL yields the following result:

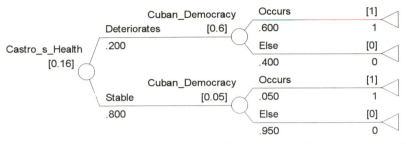

The diagram above indicates all the conditional probabilities included in the calculation and that the expert's subjective estimate for the probability that democratic reforms prevail in Cuba next year is 16%.

The following steps summarize the procedure for using decomposition to help determine the probability of an event:

Steps for Determining the Probability of an Event Using Decomposition

1. IDENTIFY CONDITIONING EVENTS: Specify any particularly salient event(s) which could increase (or decrease) the likelihood that the event of interest occurs.

2. SPECIFY FAULT TREE AS AN INFLUENCE DIAGRAM: Prepare an influence diagram that specifies the time order and dependency among uncertain events. The event of interest should be the last event at the far right of the diagram and should have influence arrows pointing to it, but no arrows pointing away from it.

3. SPECIFY CONDITIONAL PROBABILITIES: Identify the conditional probabilities associated with each uncertain event based on its place in the fault tree. (This is straightforward in DPL. To perform this step by hand it is necessary to first convert the influence diagram into a decision tree.)

4. CALCULATE THE PROBABILITY: Determine the probability of the event of interest as a function of the conditional probabilities specified. (In DPL, this involves attaching an objective node to the end of the fault tree, specifying that the objective value equals one if the event occurs and zero otherwise, and solving the problem. The expected value provided by DPL is equal to the probability of the event of interest.)

FORECASTING OPERATIONAL MEASURES

A useful forecast will provide both the probabilities of each possible outcome for each uncertain event, and an indication of how each final outcome compares according to the various operational measures included in the analysis (see Chapter Two). Predicting the future can be very difficult. Experts employ several techniques to express their uncertainty about the future. One technique is the identification and inclusion of uncertain events. These allow the expert to indicate the conditions under which a specific outcome will occur.

Another approach is to specify a range of plausible values. This range forms the basis for subsequent sensitivity analysis as described in Chapter Six. An expert might provide both a worst-case estimate and a best-case estimate for a parameter value in addition to the most plausible estimate. By providing a range of possible responses, the expert explicitly quantifies his or her uncertainty about the future. In effect, the expert is saying that it would be a surprise if the actual value that occurs ended up below the worst-case estimate or above the best-case estimate.

Surprises happen; worst- and best-case estimates would need to be quite extreme to guarantee that the prevailing outcome will always fall within the range specified. For an expert who frequently provides forecasts, one can talk about how often a surprise occurs. It should be relatively infrequent, perhaps one in every ten forecasts. A range of possible outcomes with an associated probability that the outcome falls within that range is called a *confidence interval*. Thus, an expert might indicate 90% confidence that the outcome will fall between the best- and worst-case estimates.

However, just because an expert says it's a 90% confidence interval does not mean that it is true. An expert's ability to provide 90% intervals can be tested by asking the expert to provide ten such estimates. On average, the true value should fall within the range of outcomes nine out of ten times. An expert who passes such a test can be said to be well *calibrated*. This means that the expert is well aware of his or her predictive abilities.

Being well calibrated does not necessarily mean that an expert is knowledgeable. Another factor of concern is the *precision* of the confidence interval, the width of the range from the best- to worst-case estimates. A wide range of possible values indicates that the individual has great uncertainty about what will happen. A narrow range indicates that the individual is confident of the prediction. However, a precise interval is not particularly useful unless the expert is also well calibrated.

Calibration

Becoming well calibrated takes experience and feedback. An individual typically becomes calibrated by providing many forecasts and verifying their accuracy over time. Unfortunately, this process can take a long time. Another approach to developing an expert's forecasting ability is to present the individual with a variety of scenarios that have already occurred, leaving off the final outcome. The expert can then provide a forecast as a 90% confidence interval. Since the expert does not know the outcome, this simulation is equivalent to predicting the future. However, in this exercise the expert can be provided with immediate feedback to determine whether the actual outcome was within the confidence interval specified.

If the expert misses on more than one out of ten cases, then the expert should try to adjust his or her forecasting technique in order to improve the level of calibration. The following game will allow you to test how calibrated you are on general-knowledge questions.

Test Your Calibration: The Almanac Game

This exercise tests your ability to provide 90% confidence intervals for general knowledge questions. The following ten questions were developed using the 1995 edition of the *World Almanac.*[7] For each question you are to provide a 90% confidence interval specifying the range in which the answer should fall. You may have a very good idea about the answer to some of the questions and less of an idea on others. The precision of your 90% confidence intervals should vary accordingly.

	Question	90% Confidence Interval: minimum maximum
1.	As of 1992, how many active members were in the Chinese armed forces?	
2.	How many passengers used Heathrow Airport in 1993?	
3.	How tall is the Matterhorn?	
4.	What is the land area of the Earth, in square miles?	
5.	What is the world's record distance in feet for the javelin throw?	
6.	What was the 1994 circulation of the Boston Globe?	
7.	What is the population of Jamaica?	
8.	How many times was "The King and I" performed on Broadway?	
9.	How long is the Rhine River?	
10.	In what year did Bobby Fisher first win the World Chess Championship?	

Check your answers at the end of the chapter. How many did you get right?

Most people are not particularly well calibrated. Few people actually score nine or ten out of ten on the Almanac Game. Most often their confidence intervals are too narrow, suggesting that they are *overconfident* about how much they really know. There are several psychological explanations for this broadly prevailing overconfidence. Each of them results from inexperience with developing such estimates and can be corrected with practice.

---

[7]Robert Famighetti (1994), *The World Almanac and Book of Facts 1995*, Mahwah, NJ, World Almanac, an imprint of Funk & Wagnalls Corporation.

Availability Bias

To develop an estimate, experts depend on their knowledge base. In the case of general-knowledge questions, this knowledge base typically derives from an individual's own experiences, which may not be representative.

Availability Bias: Estimating the Prevalence of Vegetarianism

What proportion of Americans are vegetarians? Different people will invariably specify very different estimates. A rancher who lives in cattle country might grossly underestimate the number on the false perception that if you don't know many of them they must be somewhat unusual and strange. On the other hand, an artist who knows many vegetarians might similarly assume that they comprise a substantial portion of the population. The mistake in each of these cases was assuming that the images available to the individual were typical. Both the rancher and the artist travel in particularly select circles and so their everyday experiences are not representative.

To correct for this bias, an expert might seek out survey data on which to base estimates as opposed to relying on the limited information available from personal experience. When such information isn't available, an expert might try to think about how his or her experiences might be biased. If such a bias could be substantial, then the estimate should be appropriately adjusted and a particularly wide confidence interval employed to indicate a lack of knowledge.

Anchoring and Adjusting

One way to develop a confidence interval is to anchor the range around the estimate for the expected case and then adjust it moderately by adding and subtracting a healthy chunk from it, say 20%, to arrive at a range of possible values. This approach often leads to an insufficiently wide confidence interval due to the nature of surprise. In particular, surprise often results from the occurrence of an unknown event. Thus, to develop a realistic best-case estimate an expert might visualize a scenario in which everything went very well. Similarly, an expert might consider various uncertain events that could dramatically alter the outcome to determine a worst-case estimate.

Anchoring and Adjusting: Renovating Jackson's Town Hall

The town of Jackson is currently having Town Hall renovated by Landmarks Renovation, Inc. The library has been moved into a new and larger facility and the space it formerly occupied is being converted to offices. Alex is charged with finding space for employees during the renovations and would like an estimate of how long until they can occupy the new offices.

Based on the extent of the renovations, Vanessa, the architect, estimated it would take twelve weeks of work. Alex wanted to be cautious so he suggested that they consider a range of possible completion dates. To derive his range he both added and subtracted two weeks from the estimate to suggest that the job should be done within ten to fourteen weeks. Vanessa cautioned him that this calculation was somewhat naive. If everything goes according to plan, the offices might be ready after ten weeks. However, if things go wrong, they could go really wrong: Materials could arrive late, previously unknown structural damage could be found, or the workers might become uncooperative. Any of these possibilities could add an extra month and a half to the renovation time. She suggested that a more realistic range of possible completion times was from ten to eighteen weeks.

Motivational Bias

Often estimates are biased on purpose in order to serve the interests of the expert who is providing them. A prudent decision analyst needs to decide whether to trust an expert's forecast or to revise it.

Motivational Bias: Tweed Jackets

Everyone at Scots Apparel is excited. The word is that tweed jackets will be in this fall. The company usually sells about a thousand jackets in any given year. Who knows how many they might sell this year? Kir McDougal, the president of the company, asked the head of each department what they thought. Here is what he found:

Department	Forecast
Finance	20,000
Sales/Marketing	2,000
Production	5,000
Distribution	15,000

He was not surprised at the lack of agreement. Finance is usually optimistic; they are in charge of preparing the business plan and always try to make the company's prospects look as good as possible. A strong forecast is particularly useful when trying to obtain loans.

He laughed when he saw sales/marketing's estimate. Their productivity is defined as the difference between actual sales and the official forecast. So, a low official forecast will help to make them look good and help them earn big bonuses.

Production tends to provide fairly accurate forecasts. They would like to provide a low estimate because they don't want to knock themselves out, especially if many of the jackets will be returned unsold. On the other hand, they will receive a lot of annoying last-minute orders if they grossly underestimate the demand.

Distribution likes to overestimate demand. This assures that there will be plenty of jackets available early when the orders first start to arrive and throughout the season for reorders. If there's plenty in the warehouse, they won't be stuck having to call around to find out which stores have remaining stock to supply those who have run out.

Based on this array of forecasts, Kir decided that the company will probably sell about 6,000 jackets. In the worst case, they might sell only 1,500 if the tweed jacket fad fails to materialize. If all goes well, and their jackets are aggressively promoted, they might sell as many as 15,000.

□ SUMMARY

Forecasts provide information about what will likely happen in the future, an important part of the basis of a decision. An expert derives a forecast from theory, experience, and an understanding of the particulars for the decision problem at hand. A forecast can be based on a conceptual understanding or on a precise mathematical representation of the dynamics of a situation. However, the precision of the mathematical model does not guarantee its accuracy. Both conceptual and mathematical models are often simplifications of a complex reality. As such, a forecast represents an expert's subjective best guess for the future and how it can be affected by current decisions.

A useful forecast will specify the probabilities associated with each uncertain event and how each final outcome scores according to the operational measures in the study. Sometimes an expert will be able to directly express the probability of an event (direct method). Otherwise, techniques can be used to help elicit a probability implicitly through hypothetical gambling games. In the betting method, the expert is asked to choose between betting for or against the event given specific payoff odds. In the comparison lottery method, the expert is asked to choose between betting on the event or on a wheel of fortune with a specified probability of winning.

When developing outcome estimates, it is useful to obtain a range of plausible values that could occur in order to facilitate subsequent sensitivity analysis. This range can be specified as a 90% confidence interval for which the expert would expect that the actual value occurring will be less than the worst-case value or better than the best-case value for one out of every ten such predictions made. Such subjective confidence intervals are often inaccurate because the expert bases the estimate on personal experience which is atypical (availability bias), develops a range by simply adding and subtracting a fixed percentage instead of creating actual best- and worst-case scenarios (anchoring and adjusting), or has a personal reason for shading the estimate one way or another (motivational bias).

□ EXERCISES

1. Convert the following odds into probabilities:

a. two-to-one	e. one-to-two	i. four-to-one
b. 3.5:2	f. 7:3	j. 4.5:7
c. 20:1	g. 100:1	k. 1:7
d. 3:8	h. 1:1.5	l. 1:7

2. People often express uncertainty using nonquantitative expressions such as "There's a good chance of rain today." Such expressions are often sufficiently precise for common conversation. However, more formal decision analysis requires that uncertainty be expressed in probabilities. The following list includes a variety of expressions for the likelihood of an event. Rank order the terms from most to least certain, based on your opinion. Identify what probability you feel corresponds to each. If you have the opportunity, it would be interesting to compare your probability assessments with others'.

a. good chance	f. highly unlikely	k. unlikely
b. probably	g. remote	l. possibly
c. I'd be surprised	h. likely	m. beyond a reasonable doubt
d. might happen	i. seems likely	
e. never happen	j. more than likely	

3. Develop your subjective estimates of the probability of the following events using the comparison lottery method.

    a. It rains tomorrow,
    b. A new war starts somewhere in the Middle East next year,
    c. The Loch Ness Monster exists,
    d. A cure for AIDS is discovered next year,
    e. Dell computers declares bankruptcy within five years,
    f. Inflation in Mexico remains under 20% next year,
    g. Mini-skirts become popular next year,
    h. The Dow Jones Industrial Average closes up at the end of next week.

4. Develop your subjective estimates of the probability of the following events using the betting method.

    a. Euro-Disney closes next year,
    b. Baleen whales become extinct within the next ten years,
    c. The Catholic Church allows women to become priests within the next ten years,
    d. Fifty percent of all MBA schools include instruction on the use of DPL in their curriculum within ten years,
    e. America Online is acquired next year,
    f. Israel and Palestine remain at peace for the next five years,
    g. Ghosts exist,
    h. The United States adopts universal health care within five years,
    i. Great Britain successively institutes the metric system within ten years.

5. Develop your subjective estimates of the probability of the following events using the direct method.

    a. The next generation of personal computer chips becomes available next year,
    b. A major earthquake rocks Tokyo next year,
    c. Quebec secedes from Canada next year,
    d. Unemployment in the United States is at 5% next year,
    e. There is intelligent life on other planets,
    f. A terrorist act succeeds at closing the Eurotunnel next year,

g. The yo-yo becomes popular next year.

6. Develop fault trees to help describe the circumstances under which the following events would occur. Identify your subjective estimates of the conditional probabilities depicted in the diagram and determine the probability of the overall event.

   a. Republicans win the next U.S. Presidential election,
   b. You will live to be 80 years old,
   c. China implements reforms to ensure humane treatment of women next year,
   d. Seinfeld goes off the air next year.

7. Which method for estimating subjective probability do you like best: direct, betting or comparison lottery? Why?

8. Provide 90% confidence intervals for the following uncertain quantities (see the end of the chapter for answers).

Question	90% Confidence Interval: minimum	maximum
a. What year did the movie *The Sting* receive the Academy Award for Best Picture?		
b. How many calories are there in an orange?		
c. What is the air distance from Hong Kong to Beijing?		
d. How much money did the United States spend to fight World War II?		
e. In what year was Buddhism founded?		
f. How many liters in a bushel?		
g. How many people died in airline accidents in 1993, worldwide?		
h. What was the population of the world in 1993?		
i. What is the circulation of *Time* magazine?		
j. How many hogs were there in the United States in 1994?		

☐ FOR YOUR PROJECT

1. Establish your credentials: You have three alternatives for fulfilling this activity. Choose to write one of the three following memos, or prepare one that blends aspects of all three:

   a. Are you an expert in the subject of your decision project? If so, write a short memo that describes your credentials for making a recommendation.

b. Can you become an expert in the subject of your decision project? If so, develop a plan for obtaining the expertise you need to prepare a decision. Write a short memo describing what books you will read, experts you will interview, and studies you will perform in order to obtain insight into your decision problem.

c. Are you constrained by both lack of expertise and lack of time? Then prepare a short cover letter that indicates the basis for your insight and concern for the problem and the nature of your limited level of expertise. This letter should indicate why your recommendation should be considered but that you understand that there are other important considerations to be included in any final decision.

2. Estimate the probabilities associated with each uncertain event.

3. Write brief scenarios to describe the nature of each potential final outcome. Provide 90% confidence intervals for any operational measures specified.

❐ FOR ADDITIONAL INFORMATION ON

Forecasting:

Brewer, Garry D. and Peter DeLeon. 1995. *The Foundations of Policy Analysis.* Homewood, IL: Dorsey Press.
Clemen, Robert T. 1996. *Making Hard Decisions: An Introduction to Decision Analysis,* 2nd ed. Belmont, CA: Duxbury.
Makridakis, Spyros, Steven C. Wheelwright, and Victor E. McGee. 1978. *Forecasting: Methods and Applications.* New York: Wiley.
Marshall, Kneale T. and Robert M. Oliver. 1995. *Decision Making and Forecasting.* New York: McGraw-Hill.

Cognitive Biases and Expert Judgment:

Bazerman, Max H. 1994. *Judgment in Managerial Decision Making.* New York: Wiley.
Dawes, Robyn. 1998. *Rational Choice in an Uncertain World.* Orlando, FL: Harcourt Brace.
Kahnemann, Daniel, Paul Slovic, and Amos Tversky. 1982. *Judgment Under Uncertainty: Heuristics and Biases.* Cambridge, UK: Cambridge.
Von Winterfeld, Detlof, and Ward Edwards. 1986. *Decision Analysis and Behavioral Research.* Cambridge, UK: Cambridge.

❐ ANSWERS TO ALMANAC QUIZZES

In Text
(1) 3.03 million, (2) 47.9 million, (3) 14,690 feet, (4) 57.9 million square miles, (5) 314 feet, (6) 508 thousand, (7) 2.6 million, (8) 1,246 times, (9) 820 miles, (10) 1972.

End of Chapter Exercise
(a) 1973, (b) 60, (c) 1,217 miles, (d) $360 billion, (e) 525 B.C., (f) 35.2, (g) 801, (h) 5.58 billion, (i) 4.1 million, (j) 57.9 million.

Chapter Five
COMPARING ALTERNATIVES AND UTILITY THEORY

OBJECTIVES
After studying this chapter you should be able to

- quantify how interested a decision maker is in avoiding risk,

- quantify how much a decision maker's satisfaction increases with successive increases in wealth or improvements in any other non-monetary objective,

- create a scorecard indicating each outcome's desirability according to the various objectives of a problem,

- elicit a decision maker's tradeoffs weights, which quantify the relative importance of the various objectives,

- identify a decision maker's preferred alternative using a payoff scorecard and tradeoff weights.

The determination of the best alternative involves comparing each alternative's expected performance on each objective and analyzing the risk associated with each alternative. In many decision problems, avoiding risk can be viewed as an additional concern to be factored into the decision. This chapter starts by discussing risk as a commodity. The Chapter then examines *utility theory*, the study of how to quantify preferences, first as a discussion of individual attitudes about different amounts of money. Next, the Chapter describes how these same techniques are employed to create scales to express preferences for nonmonetary objectives.

The chapter then turns to *multi-attribute utility theory* [MAUT], the study of techniques for assessing total satisfaction by simultaneously considering two or more objectives. Sometimes, creating a *summary scorecard* that identifies the desirability of each alternative according to each objective can help the decision maker see which alternative is preferred. Other problems are too complicated for this visual approach. Another method is to calculate an index of total satisfaction for each final outcome as a weighted average of its score on each of the objectives. The weights, called *tradeoff weights*, used in this calculation are chosen to reflect the relative importance of each objective. In this manner, the most preferred alternative can be identified as the one providing the highest total satisfaction.

Eliciting Preferences: Dr. Golub's Afternoon Snack

Folk wisdom suggests that comparing different items is generally quite difficult. There is the often-used expression, "That's hard because it's like comparing apples to oranges." It is easy to decide, when you are very hungry, whether you would prefer one orange or two. However, the aphorism implies that deciding whether you would prefer two oranges or two apples is difficult.

I strongly disagree with this expression. On most days, I would much prefer a crisp, slightly-tart apple to satisfy my hunger, especially since oranges get my hands so messy. In this regard, it is straightforward to compare apples and oranges. However, my preference may differ from yours.

RISK AS A COMMODITY

Chapter One-C introduced the solution criterion of maximizing expected monetary value [EMV]. In many situations, this decision rule seems appropriate. Large businesses typically make decisions to venture into new products or open additional franchises based exclusively on EMV. The theory being that any one product or franchise might fail, but probably not all of them will. Hence, as long as any one product does not represent too large a portion of the decision maker's budget (thereby constituting a substantial risk), the profit maximizing strategy is to maximize EMV. On the other hand, there are many situations when EMV is not an appropriate decision rule, such as when the amount of money involved is substantial.

The following mystery lotteries are designed to explore such situations. Each lottery was inspired by actual decisions people routinely consider. Think about each lottery as a monetary venture and decide what you would do.

Risk as a Commodity: Mystery Lottery #1

You are faced with the following gamble. How much would you pay in order not to have to undergo this risk?

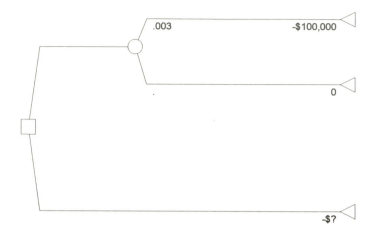

The maximum amount a decision maker is willing to pay in order not to face a risk is, in a sense, the value of the risk to that individual (actually, its negative value). It is called the *certainty equivalent* [CE] for the risky lottery. Some lotteries or risks are desirable and others are not, depending on whether one stands to gain or lose. Hence, the CE for a lottery can be either positive (if one would pay money in order to have a chance at winning) or negative (if one would be willing to pay someone else to bear the risk).

The CE does not necessarily equal a lottery's EMV. In fact, many people are willing to pay extra to avoid the possibility of a catastrophic loss. Mystery Lottery #1 represents the liability portion for an auto policy. Many people who would otherwise face this lottery are very willing to pay more than its $333 EMV to avoid the possibility of having to pay $100,000. This is why the insurance industry came into being. Insurance companies sell policies guaranteeing that they will pay in the event of an unexpected loss. By insuring many people simultaneously, a prudent insurance company can well afford to pay some claims each year. In fact, the overall proportion of drivers who will file a claim is actually quite predictable from year to year, even though it may be very difficult to predict specifically who will file a claim. Consequently, these large financial institutions can be reasonably well assured of profitability.

The difference between a decision maker's CE and the expected monetary value of a lottery is called a *risk premium*:

$$\text{Risk Premium} = \text{EMV} - \text{CE}$$

For an undesirable risk, this is the extra money the decision maker is willing to pay in order to avoid a financially risky situation. Calculate your risk premium for Mystery Lottery #1. (Note: Because you were willing to pay to get rid of the lottery, the CE is negative and your risk premium is the difference between two negative numbers.) Are you surprised at its magnitude?

There are three basic risk attitudes that can be identified by the sign of the risk premium:

- POSITIVE: When a risk premium is positive, the decision maker is willing to pay extra in order to avoid risk and is said to be *risk averse*–the larger the risk premium, the more risk averse.

- ZERO: When a decision maker's CE equals a lottery's EMV, the risk premium is zero, and the decision maker is said to be *risk neutral*. Such an individual is exclusively interested in the expected payoff associated with each alternative, in spite of any possible risk.

- NEGATIVE: There are some situations in which the decision maker would pay extra money to participate in a lottery. In which case, the risk premium is negative, and the decision maker is said to be *risk seeking*.[8] The more negative the risk premium, the more risk seeking.

Risk as a Commodity: Mystery Lottery #2
What is the most you would pay to participate in the following risky situation? Some people are not inclined to seek out gambles. If you are one of them, try turning this question around. Suppose that you have been given one chance in twenty million of winning $1 million. What is the minimum amount someone would have to pay in order to buy the lottery from you? Would you give it away for free? how about one dollar?[9]

---

[8]Kahneman and Tversky noted that individuals tend to use their current state of wealth as a reference level. Their *prospect theory* indicates that people are often much more willing to gamble on the possibility of winning substantial sums of money but are very risk averse when it comes to the possibility of losing, Daniel Kahneman, and Amos Tversky (1979), "Prospect Theory: An Analysis of Decision Under Risk." *Econometrica*, 47, 263-291.

[9]These two questions illustrate different ways of determining the value of a particular good to a decision maker: *willingness to pay*, and *compensation demanded*. In theory, a decision maker should be willing to purchase a good for at most its inherent value to him or her. Similarly, a decision maker should be willing to sell a good for no less than its value. Hence, any decision maker's maximum willingness to pay and minimum compensation demanded should both equal the inherent value of a good to him or her. However, in practice people become attached to things that they already own and minimum compensation demanded typically exceeds maximum willingness to pay.

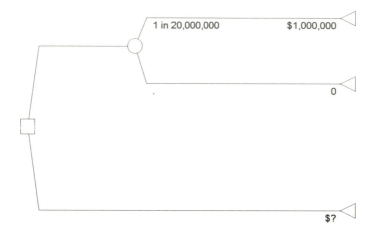

The chance of becoming instantly wealthy is very attractive to many people. These people tend to be willing to pay a dollar or two to play the lottery on a regular basis, even though the EMV for this particular lottery is only five cents. Calculate your risk premium for Mystery Lottery #2. Clearly, lottery players are not trying to maximize EMV; rather, their risk premiums are negative, and they are risk seeking. Such behavior is not an aberration, either. There are numerous ongoing million-dollar lotteries and they tend to provide substantial income to the organizations that run them. More broadly, most games of chance–such as roulette, slot machines, and horse racing–are designed so that on average most players lose and the house makes money overall. Even so, people are continually willing to gamble given the prospect of a substantial win.

Risk as a Commodity: Mystery Lottery #3
What is the most you would pay to participate in the following lottery?

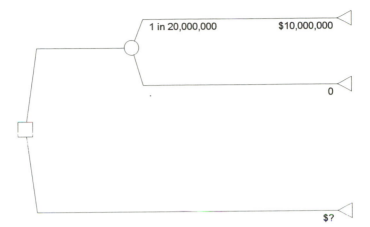

Calculate your CE for Mystery Lottery #3. Since the jackpot is larger than in Mystery Lottery #2, your CE should be larger. Is it ten times larger? Most people would not pay ten times as much for this lottery, even though its EMV is ten times larger. Most people would like to be wealthy and thus desire a million dollars. However, the additional satisfaction obtained from successive millions of dollars does not tend to increase one's happiness as much as the first million. Economists refer to this phenomenon as *diminishing marginal returns to utility*. The figure below indicates how utility typically increases with wealth. The increase in happiness from $0 to $1 million is much larger thal the increase from $1 to $2 million and even larger than the increased happiness associated with subsequent potential winnings.

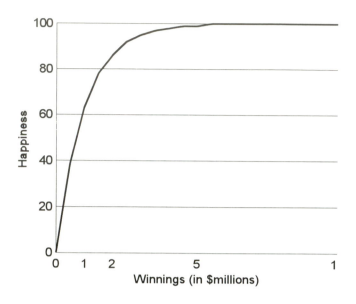

Diminishing Marginal Returns to Utility for a Lottery

CONSTRUCTING A UTILITY SCALE FOR MONEY

The previous section presented an important limitation to maximizing EMV as a decision rule. The satisfaction, also called *utility*, associated with an outcome is not always proportional to the amount of dollars received. When it is not, a more appropriate decision rule is to choose the alternative that maximizes the *expected utility* [EU], the average utility associated with an alternative.

To maximize EU, the decision analyst must convert all dollar values into their associated utilities and then employ the same procedure presented in Chapter One-C to maximize EMV. In this case, however, the procedure maximizes EU. This process can be straightforwardly performed in an influence diagram by adding an objective node after the objective money as illustrated below for the basic risky decision problem:

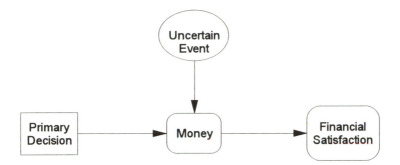

In this way, money serves as the operational measure of the outcome and financial satisfaction is the ultimate objective affected by money. The formula associated with the new objective must specify how financial satisfaction varies with wealth. The utility of an amount of money, x, is written as U(x), and reads, "the utility of x."

The correspondence between dollars, (x), and satisfaction, U(x), such as is illustrated in the graph of diminishing marginal returns to utility for a lottery, is called a decision maker's *utility scale*. This section presents several approaches for eliciting a utility scale from a decision maker. A utility scale can be developed for someone other than the decision maker. However, the role of the decision analyst is to help the decision maker come up with a best course of action based on the decision maker's preferences. Since utility is subjective, such curves will vary across decision makers.

To create a utility scale involves identifying the decision maker's relative utility for individual dollar amounts, one at a time, over the range of all possible dollar values that could result in a decision problem.[10] By convention, these utilities are expressed on a scale from 0 to 100 points. Zero represents the utility for the worst financial situation, which corresponds to the least amount of money. One hundred represents the utility for the best financial situation.

---

[10]Economists (and others) often assume that utility scales follow a specific shape such as $U(x) = x^c$ or $U(x) = (1 - e^{-x/c})$. Instead of estimating points on the utility scale, they estimate the value of the parameter c, which specifies the shape of the entire utility scale.

Equivalence Lottery Method for Eliciting a Utility Scale

Two of the approaches for eliciting utility scales require asking the decision maker to choose between a gamble and a sure thing. This decision is called an *equivalence lottery*, and is illustrated below as a decision tree:

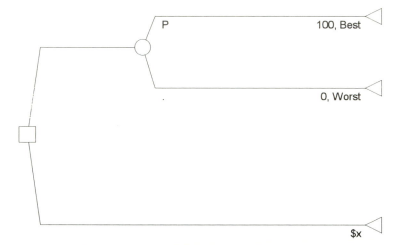

The gamble presents the decision maker with the opportunity to win the best possible outcome, which has the associated utility of 100 points. The probability of winning the best outcome is denoted as P. On the downside, losing results in receiving the worst possible outcome, which has a utility of 0 points. Alternatively, the decision maker can choose to receive a fixed amount of money, $x.

The goal of these elicitation methods is to identify a series of paired values, (P,x) for which the decision maker is indifferent between the lottery and the guaranteed money. For each such lottery, the amount of money guaranteed represents the associated CE. Each pair of values implicitly identifies another point on the utility scale.

Both of these elicitation techniques start by specifying a set of values P and x and asking the decision maker which is preferred, the lottery or the guaranteed money. If the decision maker is indifferent between the two, then this step is done, and another point on the utility scale has been found. Typically, however, the decision maker has a specific preference. In this case, the equivalence lottery is modified, perhaps several times, to find another pair of values (P,CE) for which the decision maker is indifferent. The two elicitation methods differ as to how the equivalence lottery is adjusted. In the *P-Varying Equivalence Lottery Method*, the amount of guaranteed money, x, is varied until an appropriate value is found for a specific probability, P. Alternatively, in the *CE-Varying Equivalence Lottery Method* the value of P is varied until an appropriate value is found for a specific guaranteed amount of money, x. The following description summarizes the step-by-step procedure for eliciting a utility scale using an equivalence lottery:

Steps for Eliciting a Utility Scale by the Equivalence Lottery Method
1. DETERMINE RANGE OF OUTCOMES: Identify the best and worst possible monetary outcomes.

2. CREATE A 0–100 UTILITY SCALE: Assign a utility score of 0 to the worst and 100 to the best outcome. Mathematically, this assignment is written as U(Worst) = 0, and U(Best) = 100. Start a graph of utility as a function of money and plot these first two extreme points.

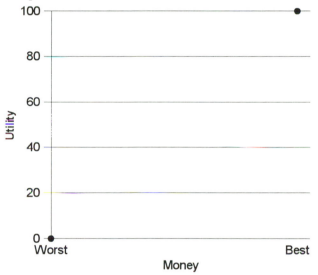

3. DETERMINE INTERMEDIATE VALUES: Repeat the following steps to identify a series of points on the utility scale:

   a. IDENTIFY A (P,CE) PAIR: For the P-varying approach, identify the CE for the following lottery (for the CE-varying approach, identify the value P for a specific value of x):

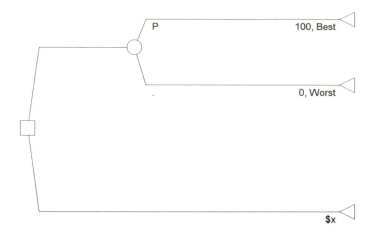

b. DETERMINE U(CE): The fact that the decision maker is indifferent between the CE and the lottery implies that their utilities are the same. This equivalence yields another point on the utility scale according to the following formula:

$$U(CE) = P \times U(Best) + (1 - P) \times U(Worst)$$

$$U(CE) = P \times 100$$

c. PLOT THE POINT: Add the data point to the graph.

d. SELECT A NEXT P VALUE: Select an area of the curve which needs further definition. For the P-Varying approach, identify a level of utility that lies within this region of the scale. The next P value to consider is the one corresponding to this utility. For example, a utility of 70 points corresponds to a probability P = 70%. (For the CE-Varying approach, select another guaranteed dollar amount.)

4. CREATE A CONTINUOUS CURVE: Draw lines connecting the points on the utility scale.

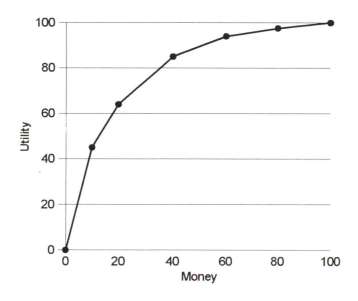

P-Varying Equivalence Lottery: Kevin's Career Choice, Part I
Kevin will be finishing his MBA in accounting at a top business school this spring. He has numerous job offers. In thinking about his career and his life, he has decided that his most important objectives are salary, location, and company product. He feels that it is important to make a good salary but that beyond some point additional income is not that important. However, after his investment of time and money in his education he would not want a low-paying job. To understand his feelings about salary more precisely, he decided to create a utility scale.

The highest-paying job offered $90,000 per year, to start; and the lowest offered $45,000. He had not ruled out the $45,000 offer because it was from a small computer company located in Boston, which sounded interesting. Using this initial information he created the following graph:

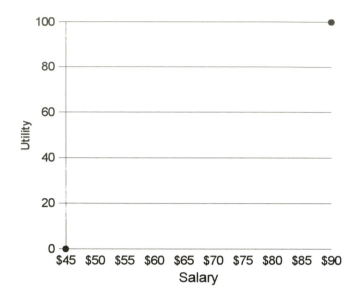

Then, he considered the following lottery:

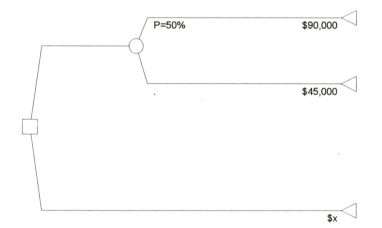

Kevin reasoned to himself that gambling on salary was not something he wanted to do, and that he would accept a reasonable sure thing like $60,000 instead. Then he thought, "How about $50,000?" To this he reasoned that $50,000 is really not that much better than $45,000, in which case he would go for the gamble. He would not go for $55,000, either, but $58,000 was high enough to tempt him. This reasoning led him to conclude that $58,000 had a utility of 50 points and he added it to his utility curve as follows:

points and he added it to his utility curve as follows:

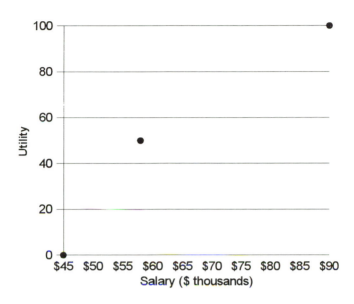

He next examined a probability of 75%, in order to fill in the upper portion of his utility curve.

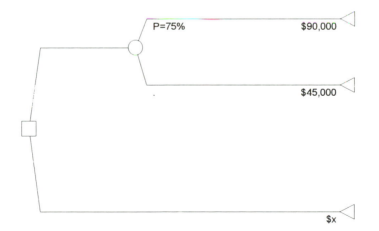

Kevin reasoned that 75% is not quite a sure thing but a very good bet; still, he would prefer a sure thing of $80,000, which is very close to $90,000, anyway. Even $70,000 would be better than the risk of making only $45,000. However,

$65,000 was as low as he would go. If he could only earn $60,000, he would prefer a risky job where he would probably receive $90,000. He concluded that $65,000 had a utility of 75 points.

Then he examined a probability of 25%, to fill in the lower portion of his utility curve. He reasoned that the lottery looked like a job with a chance of a very high salary, but one in which the greatest probability was the lower wage of $45,000. This did not sound very good. A sure thing of $60,000 sounded better, even $55,000. However, less than $55,000 was not worth thinking about. At least with the lottery, there's a chance of high pay. He concluded that $55,000 had a utility of 25 points and updated his utility curve as follows:

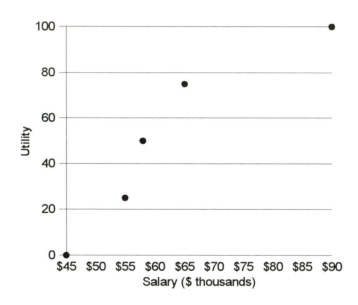

At this point, Kevin felt that he understood his feelings. Somewhere between $55,000 and $65,000 was a good comfortable salary. If he earned less than $55,000, he would be dissatisfied and probably continue to search for a new job. If he earned over $65,000 he would be financially quite content. He connected the dots on his final utility scale as follows:

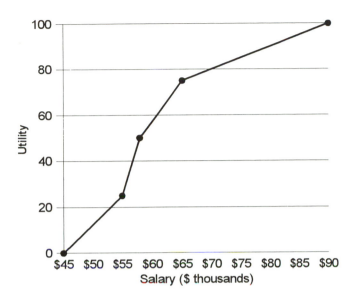

Direct Method for Eliciting a Utility Scale

The direct method differs from the preceding methods in that the decision maker specifies a subjective utility on a scale from 0 to 100 for various monetary outcomes without the use of an equivalence lottery.

Steps for the Direct Method for Eliciting A Utility Scale

1. DETERMINE RANGE OF OUTCOMES.

2. CREATE A 0–100 UTILITY SCALE: U(Worst) = 0, and U(Best) = 100.

3. DETERMINE INTERMEDIATE VALUES: Repeat the following steps for various monetary values until the utility curve seems sufficiently precise. A value halfway between the worst and the best is often a convenient starting point.

   a. DETERMINE A DATA POINT: Ask the decision maker to provide a subjective utility for the monetary value as compared to the best and worst possible outcomes.

   b. PLOT THE POINT.

   c. SELECT NEXT MONETARY VALUE.

4. CREATE A CONTINUOUS CURVE.

Risk Attitudes

The shape of a utility scale reveals a decision maker's risk attitude at a glance. The figure below illustrates the three general types of curvature. A person who is risk neutral cares equally about each dollar. This individual's utility curve follows a straight line indicating that each subsequent dollar increases utility by exactly the same amount (see the middle curve in the figure below). For these individuals, maximizing EMV is a reasonable decision rule. In fact, it is equivalent to maximizing EU. For risk-neutral decision makers, the alternative that provides the largest EMV will also maximize EU.

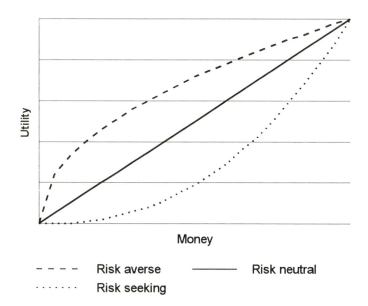

Three Risk Attitudes

A decision maker who is dissatisfied with the current situation tends to have a steep increase in overall satisfaction as wealth increases (see the lower curve in the figure above). This curve indicates that successive financial improvements lead to greater and greater increases in satisfaction. A utility scale that curves upward is called *convex*. Another way to distinguish a convex curve is that it looks like a cup that could hold water in a single pool. Individuals with convex utility scales are risk seeking.

Lastly, there is the decision maker who is generally financially satisfied. For this individual, successive increases in wealth lead to smaller and smaller improvements in satisfaction (see the upper curve in the figure above). This person's utility scale curves to the right and looks like a convex curve upside down. This shape is known as *concave*. Individuals with concave utility scales are risk averse.

Not everyone's utility scale is only concave, convex or linear. Sometimes the shape of the curve changes as wealth increases. In the case study of Kevin's career choice presented above, his utility scale followed an *s-shape*, which is quite typical. If Kevin received a low salary (substantially below his $60,000 threshold) he would be financially dissatisfied and amenable to taking risks in the hope of increasing his wealth. In this situation, his utility scale is convex. On the other side, for salaries well above Kevin's threshold his utility scale is concave. Once Kevin is making an adequate salary he would likely avoid risks to his salary.

UTILITY SCALES AND NONMONETARY OBJECTIVES

Utility scales were originally developed as a way to express how satisfaction varies with wealth. However, the same procedures can be used to develop scales for measuring how satisfaction varies with nonmonetary objectives, including such diverse concerns as commute time, warehouse space, number of injuries per year, air quality, recreational opportunities, morale, and a company's good name.

Some nonmonetary objectives have a natural order of the fewer the better (such as number of injuries); with others, it's the better (such as warehouse space). These objectives are called *nonmonetary quantities*. A decision analyst follows much the same procedure for developing a utility scale for a nonmonetary quantity as for developing a scale for money. Other nonmonetary objectives do not seem to have such an order (such as morale or a company's good name). These objectives are called *intangible concerns*. The procedure for developing a utility scale for intangible concerns is slightly different from the procedure for monetary and nonmonetary quantities. The distinction between nonmonetary quantities and intangible concerns is not always a sharp one. In terms of developing a utility scale, any nonmonetary quantity can be analyzed as an intangible concern.

Nonmonetary Objectives: Relocating Alpha Brokerage Services, Part II
One reason not to move the company from Manhattan to New Jersey is that it will cause disruption. This idea of disruption could be quantified as the number of employees who would have to relocate, although this measure seems incomplete. Disruption could be quanitified as a combination of factors including employee relocation, customer notification, time spent moving, difficulty getting the phone system set up, and so forth. This exercise, however,

appears tedious. Moreover, there are only three locations being considered and the board of directors has a clear sense of just how disruptive a move would be. Conqequently, they decided to treat disruption as an intangible concern. In this manner, the extensive work involved in specifying an operational measure or group of measures was avoided.

The following steps summarize the procedure for identifying a decision maker's utility scale for a nonmonetary objective:

Steps to the Equivalence Lottery Methods for Eliciting a Utility Scale for Nonmonetary Objectives

1. DETERMINE RANGE OF OUTCOMES: Identify the best and worst possible outcomes. For intangible concerns, rank order the list of outcomes according to the objective of interest. This step is unnecessary for most non-monetary quantities for which the more (or less) the better defines a natural rank order.

2. CREATE A 0–100 UTILITY SCALE: Assign a utility score of 0 to the worst and 100 to the best outcome. For nonmonetary quantities, start a graph of utility as a function of the objective and plot the two extreme points. For intangible concerns, keep a table identifying the utility associated with each possible outcome.

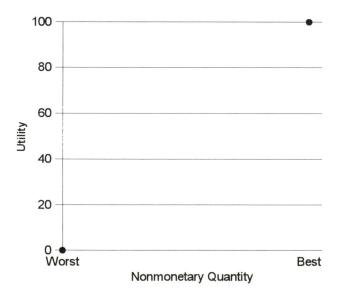

Final Outcome	Utility
Best	100
Worst	0

3. DETERMINE INTERMEDIATE VALUES: Successively vary the value of
    P or of the nonmonetary objective and repeat the following steps. For
    intangible concerns, the CE-varying approach should be used.

    a. IDENTIFY A (P,CE) PAIR: Identify the certainty equivalent for a
        lottery with probability P between the best and the worst possible
        outcomes (or the P value for a given value of the nonmonetary
        objective).

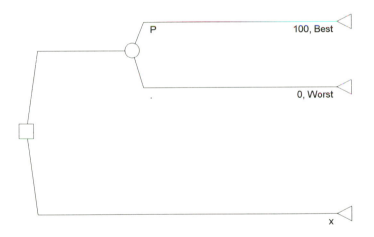

    The lottery and the CE have the same utility, which implies
    $U(CE) = P \times 100$.

    b. RECORD THE POINT: For nonmonetary quantities, plot each data
        point on the utility scale. For intangible concerns, note the utility
        associated with each outcome in a table.

    c. SELECT A NEXT P VALUE.

4. CREATE A CONTINUOUS CURVE: For nonmonetary quantities, the
    utility scale can be represented as a continuous curve. For intangible
    concerns, a table or bar graph can be used to present the preference
    information.

The direct method can be similarly adapted to develop utility scales for nonmonetary objectives.

Nonmonetary Utility Scales: Kevin's Career Choice, Part II

Kevin created the following summary scorecard to describe his job offers according to his key objectives:

Offer	Location	Industry	Salary
A	Boston	Computers	$45,000
B	Boston	Finance	$70,000
C	Boston	Retail	$50,000
D	New York City	Retail	$55,000
E	New York City	Finance	$90,000
F	Washington, DC	Telecommunications	$70,000
G	Washington, DC	Finance	$65,000
H	Washington, DC	Computers	$50,000
I	Washington, DC	Computers	$55,000

In preparation for developing an overall score for each job offer, he set out to prepare utility scales for location and industry. The first step was to rank order the choices for each objective. Regarding location, Boston was his first choice, followed by Washington, DC, and New York City. With respect to industries, computers was his favorite, followed by telecommunications, retail, and finance.

Next, he decided to create a utility scale for location using the direct approach. His first choice, Boston, received 100 points and his third choice, New York City, received 0. He next thought about whether Washington, DC, was more like New York City or Boston. He decided it was much more like Boston and that it should therefore receive well over 50 points. However, he didn't think it was as quaint, it was not as close to skiing, and it seemed more like a bustling city than Boston, although not as bustling as New York City. So he decided to award Washington, DC, 80 points on the utility scale for location. (Note: Kevin's subjective ratings are by no means universal. Other decision makers would rate these cities differently.)

Boston	100
Washington, DC	80
New York City	0

Lastly, he decided to create a utility scale for industry using the CE-Equivalence Lottery Approach. Computers, his first choice, received 100 points and finance 0 points. Then he considered the following lottery to determine his utility for telecommunications:

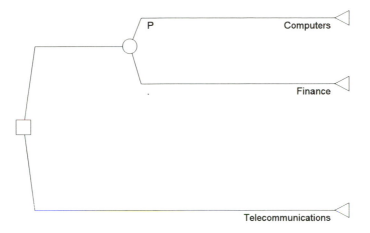

He reasoned that finance wasn't bad, but he had a strong interest in computers. Telecommunications used a lot of computers. Hence, if the chance of ending up in finance was substantial he would take the certain job in telecommunications. He decided that anything less than 97% certainty of a job in the computer industry and he would take the telecommunications job. This implied that the utility of the telecommunications industry was 97.

With regard to the retail industry job he considered the following lottery:

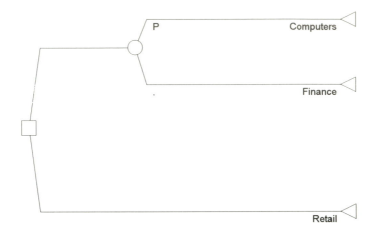

This was hard, he thought. He really wanted the computer job and would take the gamble as long as his chances were strong. Certainly, he would take a 50% risk, even a 40% or 30% risk. However, much less than that and he could pretty much count on a job in finance. How did he feel about retail compared to finance? Retail seemed much more interesting to him because it involved a physical product, but it wasn't computers. He decided that he was indifferent between a 25% chance of a job in computers versus a sure thing in the retail industry. This implied a utility of 25 for the retail industry.

Computers	100
Telecommunications	97
Retail	25
Finance	0

Having completed three individual utility analyses, Kevin was eager to use multi-attribute utility theory to identify his overall most preferred alternative.

THE SUMMARY SCORECARD

Smaller problems involving multiple objectives can often be resolved by inspecting a scorecard or table indicating each alternative's desirability according to each objective. The figure below presents the structure of a scorecard with the various alternatives along the horizontal access and the objectives along the vertical access. Uncertainty can greatly complicate a scorecard. The scorecard must provide a separate column associated with each final outcome that might prevail for each alternative. When there is no uncertainty, there is only one final outcome to consider for each alternative. In which case, the distinction between alternatives and outcomes is unnecessary. The cell entries indicate the utility of each final outcome for each objective.

	Alternative 1		Alternative 2		. . .	Alternative J
Final Outcome	1A	1B	2A	2B		
Probability	P_1	$(1 - P_1)$	P_2	$(1 - P_2)$		
Objective 1						
Objective 2						
. . .						
Objective I						

The Structure of a Summary Scorecard

The decision maker may be able to choose an alternative by simply examining a clearly organized summary scorecard. This technique is most likely to be effective when the scorecard is small, perhaps when it contains no more than four alternatives and three objectives. More than one final outcome associated with each alternative also greatly complicates a scorecard making a problem difficult to solve by inspection. The human mind is capable of juggling only so many factors at one time.

A Summary Scorecard: Relocating Alpha Brokerage Services, Part III
Alpha Brokerage Services created the following scorecard for the three locations
under consideration: their present site in Manhattan, Princeton, and Trenton.

	Manhattan	Princeton	Trenton
Operating Expenses	0	45	100
Relocation Expenses	100	10	0
Disruption	100	0	0
Maintaining Quality Staff	100	60	0
Attracting Customers	100	70	0

Their analysis suggested that the only reason to move from Manhattan is to
save on operating expenses. Princeton would allow them to maintain quality
staff and attract customers, however, the potential savings on operating expenses
is not as great as with relocating to Trenton. Locating the company in Trenton
would present greater difficulties with attracting both staff and customers.

The board of directors found the scorecard to be useful but inconclusive. The
question in their mind is, "Exactly how much savings could be achieved by
moving?" As a result of their inquiry, they developed a supplementary scorecard
indicating the expected operating costs and relocation expense for each location.
They chose not to detail the information about the other objectives sensing that
their subjective assessments were adequate. They had a pretty good sense of
what it would be like trying to work at each location.

	Manhattan	Princeton	Trenton
Annual Operating Expense	$45 million	$39 million	$25 million
Relocation Expense	$0 million	$10 million	$10 million

Based on this supplemental table and the scorecard of utilities, the board is leaning toward remaining in Manhattan, in spite of the potential savings in operating expenses. To further understand their sentiments they decided to develop tradeoff weights.

TRADEOFF WEIGHTS

Tradeoff weights provide a quantitative expression of a decision maker's priorities in terms of how much weight should be placed on each objective. This section will first describe their use and then present alternative methods for eliciting them from a decision maker. These weights can be thought of as the proportion of a decision maker's total concern placed on each objective. In this regard, tradeoff weights can be represented as portions in a pie chart, as in the figure below. The area associated with each objective indicates the relative amount of concern it occupies. Objective 1 accounts for 50% of the decision maker's concern, which is twice the priority associated with either Objective 2 or Objective 3.

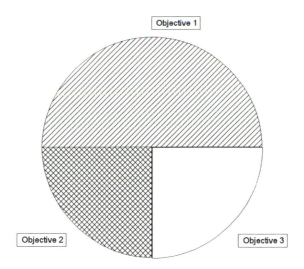

Pie-Chart Expression of Tradeoff Priorities

Tradeoff weights are used to calculate the total satisfaction for each outcome according to the following formula. (Note: In larger multi-objective decision problems that include general categories in addition to objectives and total satisfaction, as discussed in Chapter Two, this same procedure must be followed to obtain a score for each general category and then for a score on total satisfaction.)

$$\begin{bmatrix} \textbf{Total} \\ \textbf{Satisfaction} \end{bmatrix} = w_1 \times U(obj. 1) + w_2 \times U(obj. 2) + \dots + w_I \times U(obj. I)$$

Where,
w_i = weight associated with objective i
$U(obj. i)$ = an outcome's score on objective i

Total satisfaction is thus a weighted average of each outcome's desirability across all objectives, where the weights represent each objective's relative importance. This formula is called an *additive utility function,* since the utilities of each outcome are weighted and then added together. (When using DPL, this formula is typically entered in the total satisfaction element of the influence diagram, as described in Appendix A.)

The additive utility function for total satisfaction makes a very specific assumption about the relationship between the various objectives. It assumes that a decision maker's satisfaction on each objective is independent of satisfaction on every other objective. Any other assumption about interactions among objectives leads to a more complicated formula for total satisfaction and a more involved elicitation process to identify the weights. For many decision problems, the assumption of independence among objectives is quite reasonable. However, this is not always the case. For example, consider the decision of choosing among various job offers. Two primary objectives in this case are location and money. However, one's money may not go as far in some places as in others. Earning a modest salary might be perfectly acceptable when living in Seattle, but wholly unacceptable in San Francisco where the cost of living is much higher. (A thorough discussion of how to specify alternative formulas for total satisfaction to capture such interaction effects is beyond the scope of this book.)

However, there are other ways to deal with interactions among objectives. One way is to eliminate them, if possible. For example, eliminating the moderate-salary job offer in San Francisco from the analysis yields a decision problem in which the assumed independence among alternatives is reasonable. This approach is quite reasonable if the alternative probably would not be identified as the best solution.

Another way is to ignore the interactions, at least for the moment. In the job offer example, this approach would be quite reasonable, again, if the moderate-salary job offer in San Francisco is unlikely to be judged best. The moderate-salary job offer in San Francisco is unlikely to be judged best. The possible imprecision in the utility function will be revisited in the process of selecting an alternative (see Chapter Six).

The remainder of this chapter presents three alternative approaches to eliciting tradeoff weights for total satisfaction expressed as an additive utility function: direct assessment, swing weighting, and equivalence lottery.

Direct Method

The direct method provides a straightforward procedure for identifying a decision maker's priorities when the decision maker is comfortable with quantitatively expressed preferences. The following steps summarize the procedure:

Steps to the Direct Method for Eliciting Tradeoff Weights

1. PRIORITIZE OBJECTIVES: To identify the importance of each objective, think about how much better the best possible outcome is compared to the worst. Based on these differences in satisfaction, rank order the objectives from the one that provides the most satisfaction down to the least. The number-one objective is the one associated with the largest range. It is important to note that an objective's priority reflects <u>both</u> the importance of the objective and the range of possible outcomes. An objective should be assigned a very low priority if all of the possible outcomes are about equally desirable.

2. COMPARE OBJECTIVES: Compare each objective to the most important objective. (Note: Actually, any of the objectives can serve as the standard but the most important one seems like a natural choice.)

    a. Identify the relative importance of each objective priority as compared to the standard. For example, the number-one objective might be twice as important as the second-most-important objective and three-and-a-half times as important as the next.

    b. Express the relative priority as a mathematical equation. For example, a first priority that is twice as important as a second priority implies $w_1 = 2 \times w_2$.

3. IDENTIFY THE IMPLIED TRADEOFF WEIGHTS: Step 2 provides a series of mathematical equations representing the relationships between the various priorities. There should be one equation fewer than the total number of objectives. One more relationship is necessary in order to solve this system of equations for unique tradeoff weights. This final equation expresses that a decision maker's attention to the various objectives must comprise exactly 100% of his or her concern.

$$w_1 = r_2 \times w_2$$
$$w_1 = r_3 \times w_3$$
$$. \quad . \quad .$$
$$w_1 = r_I \times w_I$$

$$w_1 + w_2 + \ldots + w_I = 100\%$$

Where,

r_i = the relative importance of objective i as compared to the standard
I = total number of objectives

A straightforward approach to solving this system of equations involves successive substitution:

a. Reverse the first $(I - 1)$ equations to identify each weight in terms of w_1:

$$w_2 = w_1/r_2$$
$$w_3 = w_1/r_3$$
$$. \quad . \quad .$$
$$w_I = w_1/r_I$$

b. Substitute each comparison equation into the final equation to identify the relative importance of the number-one priority.

$$w_1 + w_2/r_2 + \ldots + w_I/r_I = 100\%$$

which implies,

$$w_1 = \frac{100\%}{\left(1 + \dfrac{1}{r_2} + \ldots + \dfrac{1}{r_I}\right)}$$

c. Use the reversed comparison equations from step 3a to identify each of the other tradeoff weights.

$$w_2 = w_1/r_2 \quad . \quad . \quad .$$

Identifying tradeoff weights using the direct approach can be facilitated with a pie chart, such as the one presented earlier in this section. In this manner, the decision maker expresses the relative priority of each objective as the portion of the pie it consumes. Some decision makers are graphically oriented and can manipulate a pie chart until the priorities seem appropriate. These same decision makers may have difficulty identifying their priorities as percentages off the top of their heads.[11]

Direct Assessment of Tradeoff Weights: High School Violence

Franklin D. Roosevelt High School was recently jarred by an incident in which one student shot and killed another during lunch break, apparently for showing a lack of respect. Parents, members of the community, and administrators were all grieved and determined to do something about violence in the school. The alternatives considered included installing metal detectors at the entrances, teaching dispute resolution, and, of course, doing nothing.

The final decision lay in the hands of Principal Chan. She identified the following objectives: assuring safety within the facility, maintaining an environment conducive to learning, and saving money. She felt that a school's first priority must always be to educate. However, safety was really a key concern, especially given the recent incident. She decided that education was 1.25 times as important as safety ($w_e = 1.25 \times w_s$). Fiscal responsibility was also essential, given the weak local economy. A manufacturing facility in the next town recently closed, and there was talk of saving money by reducing the education budget. However, the amount of money involved in any of the antiviolence measures was really quite small compared with the objectives of maintaining safety and educational standards. She decided that education was 2.5 times as important as cost ($w_e = 2.50 \times w_c$).

Her analysis yielded the following mathematical relationships:

$$w_e = 1.25 \times w_s$$
$$w_e = 2.50 \times w_o$$
$$w_e + w_s + w_c = 100\%$$

The first two equations imply,

---

[11]A pie chart can be straightforwardly created with a computer, in a spreadsheet or statistics program. Additionally, the View Wheel feature for entering probabilities for uncertain events in DPL can be adapted to this purpose. (Use of this feature is described in Appendix A.) To use this feature, create an uncertain event and specify the name of each objective as a possible state. Next, select the node values icon, select View from the menu and Wheel from the submenu. Adjust the lines delimiting the amount of the pie associated with each objective until satisfied that it reflects the decision maker's relative priorities. When satisfied, select OK and DPL will present a decision tree indicating the proportion of the pie chart associated with each objective. This is a nonstandard use of DPL. When finished, it is advisable to delete the uncertain event used to access the pie chart feature.

$$w_s = .80 \times w_e$$
$$w_c = .40 \times w_e$$

and so,

$$w_e + .80 \times w_e + .40 \times w_e = 100\%$$

$$w_e = 100\% \div (1 + .80 + .40) = 45\%$$
$$w_s = .80 \times 45\% = 36\%$$
$$w_c = .40 \times 45\% = 18\%$$

(Note: Due to rounding errors the tradeoff weights sum to 99% instead of 100%; such small roundoff errors typically do not substantially affect calculations.)

Using a summary table of utilities Principal Chan was able to identify her preferred alternative as follows:

	Metal Detectors	Dispute Resolution	Do Nothing	Tradeoff Weights
Education	0	100	65	.45
Safety	100	80	0	.36
Cost	0	35	100	.18
Total Satisfaction	36	80	47	

$$\text{Total Satisfaction} = w_e \times U(\text{education}) + w_s \times U(\text{safety}) + w_c \times U(\text{cost})$$

and so,

U(Metal Detectors)	$= .45 \times 0$	$+ .36 \times 100$	$+ .18 \times 0$	$= 36$
U(Dispute Resolution)	$= .45 \times 100$	$+ .36 \times 80$	$+ .18 \times 35$	$= 80$
U(Do Nothing)	$= .45 \times 65$	$+ .36 \times 0$	$+ .18 \times 100$	$= 47$

Based on this analysis, the principal of Franklin D. Roosevelt High School instituted a schoolwide classroom-based program to teach dispute resolution skills.

Franklin D. Roosevelt is a fictitious high school, but the problem of violence in schools is real and under study in many school districts. The alternative each selects differs according to the size and nature of each school's violence problem and the district's values.

Swing Weighting

Many decision makers find the concept of quantifying their priorities quite foreign, at least at first. The swing weighting and equivalence lottery procedures are designed to present them with more familiar types of questions. The answers to these questions can be subsequently evaluated to determine the quantitative priorities. In the swing weighting, the decision maker compares the amount of satisfaction associated with making various possible improvements to a situation. The following steps summarize the procedure:

Steps to the Swing Weighting Method for Eliciting Tradeoff Weights

1. PRIORITIZE OBJECTIVES: Rank order the objectives from most to least important.

2. COMPARE OBJECTIVES: Compare each objective to the most important objective.

   a. IDENTIFY THE STANDARD: Consider a *worst-on-all outcome*, in which the worst outcome prevails on each objective. Next, consider the improvement achieved in going from this outcome to a *best-on-one outcome* in which the best outcome prevails on the number-one priority, but the worst prevails on all the others. This exercise identifies the qualitative importance of the most important objective and acts as the standard throughout this analysis. The following summary scorecard indicates the nature of the standard improvement.

Standard Improvement	Worst-On-All → Best-On-One Outcome	Outcome
Objective 1	0	100
Objective 2	0	0
. . .	0	0
Objective I	0	0

   b. COMPARE EACH OBJECTIVE TO THE STANDARD: For each objective other than the standard, consider a similar improvement, from the worst-on-all outcome to a best-on-one outcome. The improvement associated with receiving the best on the second objective is probably not as good as for the number-one objective. For example, the improvement associated with fully satisfying the second objective might be one-half as desirable as the standard improvement.

Improvement on Objective 2	Worst-On-All → Best-On-One Outcome	Outcome

Objective 1	0	0
Objective 2	0	100
. . .	0	0
Objective I	0	0

    c.   MATHEMATICALLY EXPRESS PRIORITY: Describe the relative improvement from worst-on-all to best-on-one for each objective as a percentage of how it compares to the standard improvement. For example, an improvement on a second priority which is half as good as the standard improvement implies $w_2 = .50 \times w_1$. In other words, there is only half as much opportunity for improvement over the range of possible outcomes on Objective 2 as there is for Objective 1. (Calculating tip: Even if you think about the improvement as a fraction or percentage of the standard improvement, it is convenient to express the improvement as its corresponding decimal proportion. In this case, one-half or 50% is expressed as .50.)

3. IDENTIFY THE IMPLIED TRADEOFF WEIGHTS: Follow the procedure for direct assessment starting with step 3b, to solve the system of equations identified in step 2.

Swing Weighting: Relocating Alpha Brokerage Services, Part IV
To quantify their feelings about relocating their company, the board of directors decided to identify tradeoff weights using the swing weighting method. At first they thought that maintaining and attracting customers should be their first priority. However, since so many of their customers transacted business over the phone, the potential loss in moving to New Jersey was actually slight. The single most relevant factor appeared to be the large cost savings that could be achieved, which they designated as their standard. Initially, they could not agree on the rest of the rank ordering and so they decided to identify the relative importance of the other objectives in the order in which they appeared in their summary scorecard.

    They started their analysis by considering the grim prospect of having to pay Manhattan-level operating costs, pay relocation expenses, and endure a major disruption, while at the same time having difficulty attracting staff and customers. They found the prospect quite ludicrous, perhaps not even worthy of their consideration. If that were the case, they might even just close down the company. However, that would be an overreaction. Trenton is the capital of New Jersey, and as such there are many potential brokerage customers and a pool of potential employees. Hence, the absolute worst outcome on all objectives presented a tenable situation, albeit one with considerable room for improvement.

    Next they thought about the improvement standard, a situation that was best on operating expenses but worst on all other objectives. The prospect of saving $20 million per year was very satisfying.

Their enthusiasm for annual savings needed to be immediately tempered by relocation expenses, which were estimated at about $10 million. Being in the finance industry, they were used to comparing different investments using net present value. (Appendix D provides additional information about these types of calculations.) If they assumed an interest rate of 10%, then an operating savings of $20 million per year was comparable to having $200 million in the bank. In other words, if they had $200 million invested at 10% per year, they would receive $20 million each year. So, the savings of the relocation expense represented only 5% of the expected savings in annual operating expenses in the long run. Thus, $w_2 = .05 \times w_1$ ($10 million ÷ $200 million = .05).

Even more than the financial expense, they were worried about the anxiety and pressure of relocation. The company was operating smoothly. As a result of relocation, some employees would leave the company, new suppliers would have to be found, and much work would be lost as employees relocated families and spent time setting up their offices. These nuisances not only represented additional possible expenses but there would be a short-term decline in morale and cooperation, which could further reduce profitability. The board thought about the best-on-one improvement associated with avoiding the relocation disruption. The thought of not having to relocate was quite attractive. However, would they endure the disruption to save $20 million per year? They decided that indeed they would. They decided that the swing from worst-on-all to best-on-one for the disruption objective improved their satisfaction 70% of the standard improvement ($w_3 = .70 \times w_1$).

Following similar reasoning, they concluded that the swing from the worst-on-one to the best-on-one outcome for maintaining staff represented 40% of the standard ($w_4 = .40 \times w_1$) and that maintaining customers was 55% of the standard ($w_5 = .55 \times w_1$).

These analyses led to the following equations:

$$w_2 = .05 \times w_1$$
$$w_3 = .70 \times w_1$$
$$w_4 = .40 \times w_1$$
$$w_5 = .55 \times w_1$$
$$w_1 + w_2 + w_3 + w_4 + w_5 = 100\%$$

This implied,

$$w_1 + .05 \times w_1 + .70 \times w_1 + .40 \times w_1 + .55 \times w_1 = 100\%$$
$$w_1 = 100\% ÷ 2.7 = 37\%$$

and further implied,

$$w_2 = .05 \times 37\% = 2\%$$
$$w_3 = .70 \times 37\% = 26\%$$
$$w_4 = .40 \times 37\% = 15\%$$
$$w_5 = .55 \times 37\% = 20\%$$

The board subsequently entered these tradeoff weights into their Summary scorecard and calculated the overall preference for each location.

	Manhattan	Princeton	Trenton	Tradeoff Weight
Operating Expenses	0	45	100	.37
Relocation Expenses	100	10	0	.02
Disruption	100	0	0	.26
Maintaining Quality Staff	100	60	0	.15
Attracting Customers	100	70	0	.20
Total Satisfaction	63	40	37	

The total satisfaction scores confirmed their sense that you can't have it all, and that remaining in Manhattan was their preference. Princeton and Trenton were overall more than one-third less desirable.

Equivalence Lottery

Expressing improvement as a percent, such as in the swing-weighting method, can appear fairly abstract and unfamiliar to a decision maker. The equivalence lottery approach uses a gamble instead. The following steps summarize the procedure:

Steps to the Equivalence Lottery Method for Eliciting Tradeoff Weights
1. COMPARE OBJECTIVES:
   a. IDENTIFY BEST-ON-ALL AND WORST-ON-ALL OUTCOMES: Consider the difference in satisfaction between an outcome that has the best value for each objective, the *best-on-all outcome*, and one that has the worst for each, the *worst-on-all outcome*. The best-on-all outcome is designated as having a utility of 100 and the worst-on-all a utility of 0.
   b. IDENTIFY EACH OBJECTIVE'S RELATIVE IMPORTANCE: For each objective, consider a best-on-one outcome that is worst on every objective except the one. Identify the probability P for which the

decision maker is indifferent between the best-on-one outcome and a gamble between the best-on-all and worst-on-all outcomes.

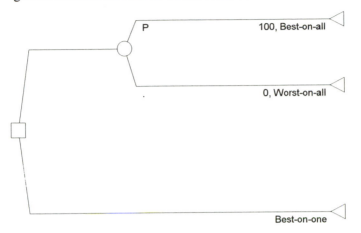

This equivalence implies a relative utility [U_i] for the objective of P × 100.

2. IDENTIFY THE IMPLIED TRADEOFF WEIGHTS: Tradeoff weights [w_i's] can be determined by normalizing the utilities so that they add up to one. To accomplish this, add up the relative utilities for all the objectives. An objective's tradeoff weight is equal to its utility divided by the sum of all of the utilities.

$$w_i = \frac{U_i}{U_1 + U_2 + \ldots + U_I}$$

Equivalence Lottery: Kevin's Career Choice, Part III
Kevin decided to use the equivalence lottery approach to identify his tradeoff weights. His worst-on-all outcome was a finance job in New York City paying $45,000. This was not his dream job, but it wasn't bad. His best-on-all outcome was a job in the computer industry in Boston, paying $90,000. Indeed, not one of his offers was simultaneously best on all objectives. Had this been the case, he would have accepted that offer.

To identify the utility associated with salary he considered a lottery with the best-on-all with worst-on-all outcomes to a sure thing of the best-on-salary job (living in New York City, working in finance, and receiving $90,000). He asked himself which he prefers, if the probability of the best-on-all outcome is 50%. The following decision tree illustrates his choice:

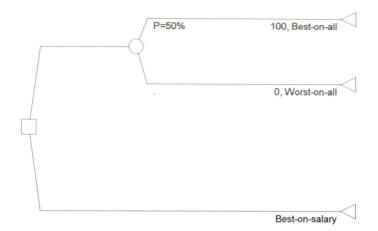

The high salary seemed very tempting and he decided he would go for that sure thing. For $P = 80\%$, the possibility of the best-on-all was tantalizing, but he still preferred receiving the high salary for sure. For $P = 90\%$, it seemed worth taking the risk. He concluded that for $P = 85\%$ he would have difficulty deciding between the gamble and the best-on-salary outcome. This indifference relationship implies that his utility for salary $U_s = 85$.

Using similar logic, he determined the utility of location, being assured that he would work in Boston, $U_l = 40$. If his probability of winning the best-on-all outcome was less than 40%, then he would settle for the best-on-location outcome. His utility for industry was $U_i = 75$. He figured that as long as he had a job in computers he could eventually work his salary up and relocate to Boston. Hence, for less than a 75% chance at the best-on-all outcome, he would settle for the best-on-industry job, working in computers.

To calculate his tradeoff weights, he first added together the relative utilities:

$$U_s + U_l + U_i = 85 + 40 + 75 = 200$$

Then he determined tradeoff weights by dividing each utility by the sum of the relative utilities:

$$w_s = U_s \div 200 = 85 \div 200 = .42$$
$$w_l = U_l \div 200 = 40 \div 200 = .20$$
$$w_i = U_i \div 200 = 75 \div 200 = .38$$

He entered the tradeoff weights into his summary scorecard and determined his overall preference for each job offer.

Offer	Location	Industry	Salary	Overall Score
A	100	100	0	58
B	100	0	80	54
C	100	25	13	35
D	0	25	25	20
E	0	0	100	42
F	**80**	**97**	**80**	**87**
G	80	0	75	48
H	80	100	13	59
I	80	100	25	64
Tradeoff Weights	.20	.38	.42	

At first he was somewhat surprised. His overall preference, by a large margin, turned out to be the telecommunications job in Washington, DC, paying $70,000 per year. Initially, this had sounded like a good offer, but it was not his best offer on any one single objective. Yet as a compromise, he preferred it by more than one-third to the next best job offer ($87 \div 64 = 1.36$). He went back and looked at the job offers to see if he could find one that was better and he really could not. He was very glad that he had performed a formal decision analysis. It helped him focus his thoughts and deal with a complicated decision. He graciously accepted the telecommunications offer and looked forward to starting work.

☐ SUMMARY

Maximizing expected monetary value is a reasonable decision rule when objectives other than money are not paramount and the amount of money involved is relatively small compared to the decision maker's budget. When larger amounts of money are involved, the risk neutral approach of maximizing EMV is less appropriate. In particular, some individuals are typically afraid of large losses and are willing to pay a premium to avoid such risks. These people are risk averse. On the other hand, often people are dissatisfied with their current wealth and are willing to pay a premium for a chance to improve their lot. These people are risk seeking. For individuals who are not risk neutral, maximizing expected utility provides a better decision rule than maximizing expected monetary value. A utility scale describes how a decision maker's satisfaction varies with monetary wealth. Such scales can be devloped using an equivalence lottery approach varying either the probability or the certainty equivalent. A direct approach can also be used. Utility scales are also used to quantify a decision maker's preference for various non-monetary objectives.

Many decisions involve selecting an alternative that is best according to more than one objective. With smaller problems, a scorecard which displays how well each alternative performs according to each objective provides a useful summary and may allow a decision maker to identify a preferred alternative. A more quantitative approach is to identify tradeoff weights which express the relative priority of each objective. These tradeoff weights–along with the individual utility scores on each objective–allow the decision analyst to calculate a score on total satisfaction for each outcome. The alternative with the highest expected total satisfaction is the decision maker's best choice. This choice maximizes the decision maker's expected utility taking into consideration possible risks and multiple objectives.

❒ EXERCISES

1. Create your own utility scale for possible salary offers using the P-varying equivalence lottery method. Consider a range of possible values based on your current employment or on your possible expectations subsequent to further education.

2. Imagine that you are in charge of marketing the latest prepared dinner for a major food manufacturer. This product might lose as much as $1 million or earn as much as $10 million in its first year. Use the CE-varying equivalence lottery method to identify your utility associated with each possible outcome over this range.

3. You have been asked to make the arrangements for a decision makers' retreat. Possible off-site locations include Honolulu, Aspen, Seattle, New York City, and Washington, DC. Identify the objectives you would use in making this decision. Use the CE-varying equivalence lottery method to identify the general desirability of each site.

4. Identify five types of jobs you would consider taking. Identify the objectives you would use in making this decision. Create a utility scale using the direct approach.

5. Which method for eliciting a utility scale do you prefer? Why?

6. Find the tradeoff weights for each set of relationships.

   a. $2 \times w_1 = w_2; 3 \times w_1 = w_3$.

   b. $w_1 = w_2; 3 \times w_1 = w_3$.

   c. $w_1 = .80 \times w_2; w_1 = .60 \times w_3$.

   d. $w_1 = w_2; w_1 = .75 \times w_3; w_1 = .40 \times w_4$.

   e. $w_1 = .80 \times w_2; w_1 = .60 \times w_3; w_1 = .45 \times w_4; w_1 = .25 \times w_5$.

7. Xenon Motors is considering several locations for their new production facility. They've identified land costs [L], workforce quality [W], and local government support [G] as their priorities. Identify their tradeoff weights based on the following: Workforce quality is the highest priority, it is 1½ times as important as land costs, and twice as important as local government support.

8. Identify the various course objectives for this class (e.g., term project, exams, homework, class participation). Use the equivalence lottery approach to identify tradeoff weights for the relative importance of each grading element, based on your own subjective opinion. Do you think others would agree with your priorities?

☐ FOR YOUR PROJECT

1. Create 0-100 utility scales for each objective in your decision problem.

2. Enter each outcome scale's score into your representation of your decision problem.

3. Create a scorecard for your decision problem. If your problem is particularly complicated, create a simplified scorecard which includes a limited number of alternatives (perhaps 4) and objectives (perhaps 3). Additionally, you might decide to further simplify the scorecard by not including any uncertain events. Instead you might consider using the most likely outcome to characterize each alternative. Choose an alternative based on this scorecard. Do you feel confident in your selection? Was this approach appropriate to your decision problem? Was this approach superficial? If so, what bothers you about your selection or the selection process?

4. Identify tradeoff weights for the various objectives in your decision problem. Enter this multi-attribute utility formula into the total satisfaction element in the representation of your problem.

5. You now have enough information to identify your preferred alternative based on your structuring of the problem, your subjective assessment of any probabilities, and your priorities and values. Calculate the alternative with the highest expected total satisfaction.

☐ FOR ADDITIONAL INFORMATION ON

Eliciting utility functions:

Clemen, Robert T. 1996. *Making Hard Decisions: An Introduction to Decision Analysis,* 2nd ed. Belmont, CA: Duxbury.

Summary Scorecards:

Patton, Carl V. and David S. Sawicki. 1993. *Basic Methods of Policy Analysis & Planning.* Englewood Cliffs, NJ: Prentice-Hall.

Cost-Benefit Analysis:

Stokey, Edith and Richard Zeckhauser. 1978. *A Primer for Policy Analysis*, New York: Norton.

Chapter Six
SELECTION AND SENSITIVITY ANALYSIS

OBJECTIVES

After studying this chapter you should be able to

- identify the extent to which a decision recommendation depends upon the various assumptions and values of the analyst,

- determine whether it would be useful to obtain additional information which would improve the accuracy of the forecast and how much it would be worth paying for such information.

By this time, the wide variety of information needed to make a decision has been gathered and folded into the analysis. It is now a time to reflect and to prepare a report to the decision maker in anticipation of moving from analysis to implementation. Selecting an alternative should be thought of as a three-part process rather than as a single event. The first part is to work with the decision model to identify a best recommendation which truly reflects the analyst's understanding of the problem and the values of the decision maker. The chapters leading up to this point have discussed how to develop an appropriate model of a decision problem. Before preparing a report, the analyst should double check everything, verifying that numbers were entered correctly and calculations performed properly. Additionally, the analyst should identify the specific assumptions behind the analysis.

The analyst need not recommend a solution just because a model suggested it was best. Quite often, the assumptions behind an analysis appear reasonable, but other assumptions would also appear reasonable. It is important to ask whether varying the assumptions in a decision analysis would result in a different alternative being identified as best. *Sensitivity analysis* is the systematic study of how the solution to a model changes as the assumptions are varied. Because such analyses are quite often phrased as "What would happen if . . ." sensitivity analysis is also known as *what-if analysis*.

The second part of the selection process is to perform sensitivity analysis to obtain a fuller understanding of the dynamics of the decision problem. An analyst is fortunate when the best alternative remains the same even when the assumptions underlying the analysis are varied. When this happens, a solution is said to be *robust*. Under these circumstances, a decision analyst can recommend an alternative with great confidence. Often, however, when the assumptions are varied, the best alternative changes. Under these circumstances, a decision analyst might wish to avoid making a firm recommendation. Instead, the analyst might present the decision maker with a list of those alternatives that score well and a description of the assumptions that favor each. Alternatively, the analyst might consider obtaining additional information before making a decision. This chapter describes how to perform sensitivity analysis and how to determine whether additional information would be worthwhile.

After performing sensitivity analysis, the analyst is in a position to recommend an alternative. (Appendix E provides an outline to assist in the preparation of a decision recommendation.) If this recommendation differs from the original alternative identified by the representation of the decision model, the analyst might cite the results of sensitivity analyses or other considerations not fully incorporated in the analysis as a basis for recommending a different solution.

Most importantly, the choice of which alternative to implement ultimately rests with the decision maker, who need not follow the decision analyst's recommendation. The third part of the selection process is for the decision maker to consider the analyst's recommendation, perhaps negotiate with the individuals who will be ultimately responsible for implementing the alternative, and determine which alternative will be implemented. This final selection might differ from the analyst's recommendation, which might also differ from the initial solution to the model of the decision problem.

SENSITIVITY ANALYSIS

The best solution identified by a model of a decision problem typically depends on the various numbers used, including probability estimates, outcome estimates, and tradeoff weights. In performing sensitivity analysis, it is useful to distinguish between the role that a number serves and its actual value. In referring to its role, a number is called a *parameter*. The statement, "The probability of cold weather is 40%," identifies the parameter the probability of cold weather. This parameter might be denoted as Pr[Cold] or simply as P. The parameter value in this case is 40%.

Sensitivity analysis asks whether the solution to the decision problem will change if the parameter values are varied. Sensitivity analysis can involve systematically varying one, two, or all the parameter values, simultaneously.

The one-parameter sensitivity analysis involves setting a parameter to a variety of reasonable levels and observing how the solution changes. A *rainbow diagram*, a graph that displays how the expected payoff and best alternative change as the parameter value is varied, provides a concise summary of the results of a one-parameter sensitivity analysis. (Appendix A describes how to create a rainbow diagram with DPL.)

One-Parameter Sensitivity Analysis: Bedford's Picnic, Part I

The Town of Bedford is planning a celebration to honor its gold-medal-winning Olympic cross-country skier. The celebration is set to be held in the town's center for the day she returns, March 15. Unfortunately, the weather report predicts that the temperature might not be conducive to an outdoor event on that day. As a backup plan, they are thinking about reserving space indoors. However, that reservation would cost additional taxpayers' money. This basic risky decision with multiple objectives can be represented by the following influence diagram. Whether they reserve the indoor space influences whether the celebration is canceled and how much money is spent.

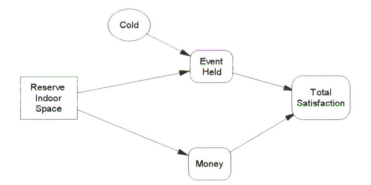

The solution to this decision problem requires the specification of two parameters: the probability of cold weather, and the tradeoff weight indicating the relative importance of holding the event to paying fees for indoor space. In analyzing this problem, Julie Bauer, the town manager, estimated there was a 40% chance of cold weather and that holding the event was twice as important as saving taxpayer's money. Hence, the tradeoff weights were ⅔ and ⅓. Note, the tradeoff weights are fully determined by the specification of the one parameter, the relative weight of each. Furthermore, since there are only two alternatives, rent the indoor space or not, the utility scales for each objective require no additional parameters. Renting space receives a score of 100 (best) on holding the event and 0 (worst) on saving money. Conversely, not renting space receives a 100 on saving money, but if it's cold out, then it receives a 0 on holding the event. The scorecard for this problem is as follows:

	Alternatives--Outcomes				
	rent space		don't rent space		
(Cold?)	Yes	No	Yes	No	
probability	.40	.60	.40	.60	
					Tradeoff
Objectives					Weights
hold event	100	100	0	100	.67
save money	0	0	100	100	.33
Total Satisfaction (by outcome)	67	67	33	100	
Total Satisfaction (by alternative)		67		73	

The results indicate that not renting space has the highest expected utility, 73 points. However, Julie noted that renting space, at 67 points, was a very close second. She wondered how her decision was affected by the probability of cold weather and the tradeoff between the two objectives and so she performed sensitivity analyses on each parameter.

She varied the probability of cold weather through the full range of values from 0.0 to 1.0, representing the range from certain warmth to certain cold. She also varied the tradeoff weight for holding the event (as compared to saving money) from 0 to 1 where 0 represents the value of saving money over all else and 1 represents the converse value of holding the event at any cost.

The rainbow diagram below indicates that if the probability of cold weather is greater than 50% then the indoor space should be rented.

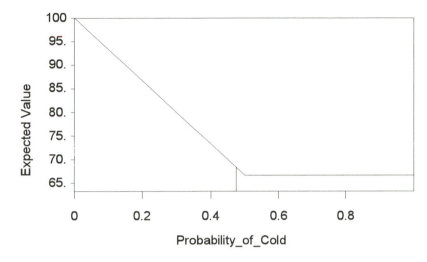

The value at which the best solution changes from one alternative to another is called a *critical point*. This point can be calculated exactly as the value for P at which the expected utility for both alternatives is the same, as follows:

$$EU[\text{Rent Space}] = EU[\text{Don't Rent Space}]$$

$$67 = P \times 33 + (1 - P) \times 100$$

$$67 \times P = 33$$

$$P = 33/67$$

$$P = 50\%$$

The rainbow diagram below indicates that as long as the tradeoff weight associated with holding the event ratio is less than .71 then the indoor space should not be rented. The critical value of .71 corresponds to the situation in which holding the event is valued 2.5 times as important as saving money.

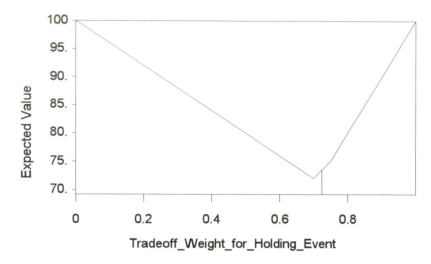

The precise critical point can be calculated by solving for the tradeoff weight (W) at which the expected utilities for both alternatives equal each other, as follows:

$$EU[\text{Rent Space}] = EU[\text{Don't Rent Space}]$$

$$W \times 100 = .40 \times (1 - W) \times 100 + .60 \times 100$$

$$W \times 100 = 40 - W \times 40 + 60$$

$$W \times 140 = 100$$

$$W = 100/140$$

$$W = .71$$

Julie pondered the situation. The difference between valuing the holding of the event 2 times as much as saving money is not very different from valuing it 2.5 times as much. She concluded that her solution to the problem was not particularly robust, especially when considering variation in tradeoff weights.

One-parameter sensitivity analyses check the robustness of the solution to variations, one parameter at a time. Sometimes, a solution will be quite robust to changes in one parameter but may vary substantially if more than one parameter is varied simultaneously. The variation in the solution as two parameters vary can be shown in a two-dimensional graph. The variation as three parameters vary, theoretically, can be shown in a three-dimensional graph. Drawing and interpreting three-dimensional graphs, however, is quite a bit more complicated than working in two dimensions. Analyzing the simultaneous variation in more than three dimensions is substantially harder. One approach to varying all parameters in a decision problem simultaneously is the multiple-perspectives sensitivity analysis, which identifies several different types of forecasters or stakeholders, the parameter values each would tend to suggest, and the solution each would recommend based on the model of the decision problem.

Two-Parameter Sensitivity Analysis: Bedford's Picnic, Part II

Julie was not completely comfortable with the results of her one-parameter sensitivity analyses. In particular, she was troubled by the fact that the best solution shifted with just a minor change in either parameter value. She thought, "What if both the probability of cold weather and the relative utility of the two objectives shift simultaneously?" To show how her decision varied with both parameters simultaneously she created the following graph.

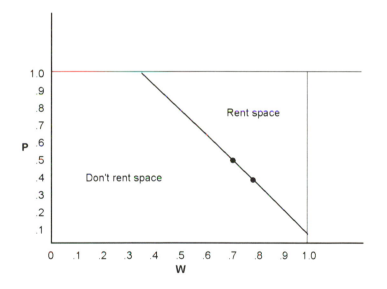

To create the graph she plotted the two pairs of critical values (P,W) she found in the previous one-parameter sensitivity analysis {(P = .5, W = .67) and (P = .4, W = .71)}. Then she drew the line defined by these two points. Lastly, she identified which alternative was preferred on either side of the line.

Julie was still uncomfortable about having to make a decision. Neither alternative–renting or not renting indoor space–clearly dominated the other. Finally, she realized that if the alternatives are comparably good then she could simply choose either. No one could fault her that she had made a bad decision. Perhaps more accurately, people were going to fault her should she fail to predict the weather accurately. Her decision was to choose which risk she wished to face: being held responsible for renting unnecessary space or for not being able to hold the event. She chose to rent the indoor space and contented herself with the fact that she had thoroughly analyzed her decision.

VALUE OF INFORMATION

Before making a recommendation, it might be useful to ponder whether there is enough information available to make an informed decision. In particular, often the outcome is highly dependent on the results of an uncertain event, such as in the basic risky decision, as illustrated in the following decision tree.

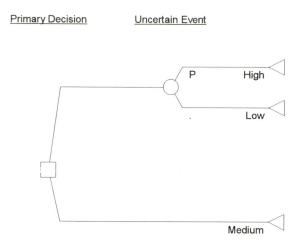

It would be preferable to know the outcome of the uncertain event in advance of making a decision. In this revised problem, the order of the uncertain event and the decision are reversed, as illustrated below:

<u>Uncertain Event</u>   <u>Primary Decision</u>

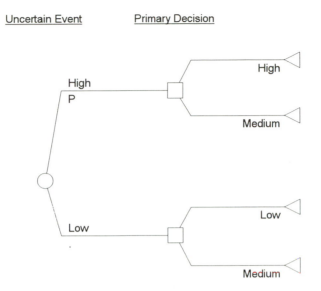

This reversed ordering assures the decision maker of always receiving the best outcome possible.

Often, a more accurate forecast of the outcome can be obtained for a price. This price might be the cost of a pilot project, a test market, a survey, or additional research. On the down side, such additional information will probably cost money. This section examines how much it would be worth paying to obtain such additional information. (The procedure for creating a perfect information decision from a risky decision in DPL is straightforward and described in Appendix A.)

It is important to distinguish two possible types of information. The first type, called *perfect information*, indicates the outcome of the uncertain event with certainty. Additional information that provides further indication of whether the uncertain event will occur, but not enough to know the final outcome with certainty, is called *imperfect information*.

The following decision tree illustrates the choice of whether to purchase perfect information, assuming it is available:

Buy Additional Information

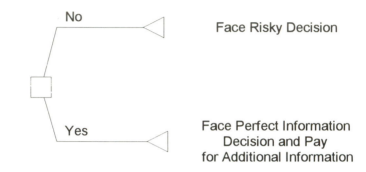

The decision to buy the additional information makes sense when the expected value of the perfect information decision is much larger than the expected value of the existing risky decision, at least as large as the price of the information. For this reason, the difference between the expected value of the perfect information and the risky decisions is called the *expected value of perfect information* [*EVPI*].

Sometimes, the information that can be purchased is less than perfect. How much is this type of information worth? One quick answer is that it is worth less than the value of perfect information. Hence, if the cost to obtain the information is higher than the EVPI, then it is not worth purchasing. A more accurate estimate can be obtained by solving a revised problem, such as the one illustrated in the figure below, and comparing the expected payoff to the original problem.

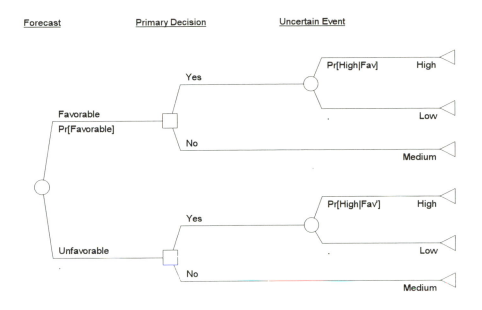

This latter approach requires that the analyst specify detailed information about the testing procedure: the various possible forecasts it might produce, the probability that it provides each, and the probabilities associated with the original uncertain event for each possible forecast. Hence, this calculation of the expected value of imperfect information is most useful when dealing with widely used tests for which these characteristics are well established.

Expected Value of Perfect Information: A Cure for Lyme Disease, Part II

Bill MacKenzie had become somewhat uncomfortable about committing Jackson Pharmaceuticals to Lyme disease research, especially because there was only a 20% chance of success. He decided to consider funding a pilot study that could determine almost certainly whether the research would find a cure. He wasn't sure how much the lab equipment would cost for such a study, but he knew it would be expensive. He decided to do an EVPI calculation to identify how much it would be worth. The following influence diagram represents the initial decision:

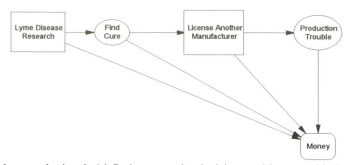

If he knew whether he'd find a cure, the decision problem would change as follows:

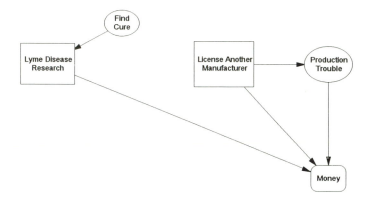

which corresponds to the following decision tree:

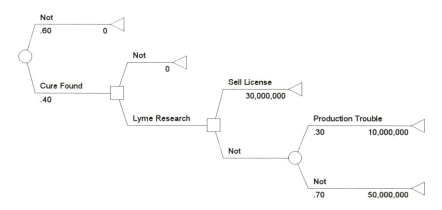

The solution of this informed decision has an expected payoff of $15.2 million, well above the $9.2 million associated with the original risky problem. Thus, it would be worth up to $6 million to know with certainty whether Jackson Pharmaceuticals could find a cure for Lyme disease.

◻ SUMMARY

The selection process involves three parts. The first is to ascertain that the model is a reasonable representation of the decision problem. The next part is to examine how the solution changes as key parameter values–such as probabilities and tradeoff weights–are varied. A solution to a problem that does not vary much is said to be robust. In this case, the analyst will probably want to recommend this solution. Otherwise, the analyst might want to recommend any of several high-scoring solutions, each of which provides a high expected utility under at least one set of reasonable assumptions.

At this time, the analyst might wish to consider obtaining additional information, if possible. This information might change a risky problem into one in which the outcome of an uncertain event is known in advance of making a decision, a perfect information problem. The expected value of perfect information [EVPI] is defined as the difference between the expected value of the problem with perfect information and the risky problem. It is worth paying up to the EVPI to obtain perfect information. Imperfect information provides further information about whether an uncertain event will occur, but does not provide enough information to reduce an uncertain event to a certainty. Imperfect information has a value somewhere between nothing and the value of perfect information. The procedure for calculating the expected value of imperfect information is more involved.

The last part of the selection process involves presenting a recommendation over to the decision maker. The decision maker considers the results of the decision analysis, factors not explicitly incorporated in the model of the decision problem or sensitivity analysis, and other issues associated with implementing the decision. The final decision as to which alternative gets implemented rests with the decision maker. The solutions identified by the model of the decision problem, the decision analyst's recommendation, and the decision maker's selection can differ from one another.

◻ EXERCISES

1. Consider Exercise 2, from Chapter One-C: Perform a sensitivity analysis for the probability of a frost ruining the crop over the range from $P = 0\%$ to 100%. Present your results as a rainbow diagram. Interpret your findings.

2. Consider Exercise 3, from Chapter One-C: Perform two sensitivity analyses, one for the probability that the product is a success over the range from $P = 0\%$ to 100%, the other for outplacement costs ranging from \$50,000 up to \$300,000. Present your results as a rainbow diagram. Interpret your findings.

3. Consider Exercise 1, from Chapter One-C: What is the largest amount of money the city should pay in order to find out with certainty whether there will be a heavy snowfall. Explain your answer.

4. Consider Exercise 4, from Chapter One-C: What is the largest amount of money the city manager should pay in order to know with certainty whether the city will receive the $300,000 in matching funds? Explain your answer.

□ FOR YOUR PROJECT

1. Reexamine the problem definition and structure of your decision problem. Are you still satisfied that you are solving the right problem and that you have a reasonable model of the decision problem? If not, make any necessary changes to your influence diagram.

2. Choose the most important uncertain event in your decision problem. If your problem does not include risk, then skip this step. Determine how much money it would be worth to know the outcome of this event with certainty. (Depending on your problem this value might be expressed in dollars or in points on the total satisfaction scale.) Is it possible to obtain this information?

3. Prepare a rainbow diagram sensitivity analysis for two of the most important parameter values in your decision problem. In this case, importance should be determined as the parameter values in which you have the least confidence.

4. Prepare a final report according to the outline provided in Appendix E.

Appendix A
A GUIDE TO DPL

OBJECTIVES
After studying this appendix you should be able to

- create an influence diagram using DPL,

- use DPL to solve a decision analysis,

- print diagrams and charts from DPL,

- use DPL to perform a sensitivity analysis, and to calculate the expected value of perfect information.

DPL is a Windows-based computer program specifically designed for solving decision problems as either influence diagrams or decision trees. Software written for the Windows operating system employs a standard format. Hence, many of the functions in the program should appear familiar. This appendix describes the basic features of DPL used to support the analyses described in this text. These analyses employ the graphical interface in the DPL Draw window that appears automatically when the standard student version of DPL is selected. (In the advanced and professional versions of DPL this feature is accessed by selecting draw from DPL's main menu.) Additional help with these and other features can be obtained from the help menu. This feature allows the user to request information about a topic from a table of contents, and to search a list of keywords to identify a topic. It also provides advice as to how to use the help feature.

This appendix is organized according to the order in which the various DPL features would be accessed to create an influence diagram. Details for creating an influence diagram for the following tutorial example are interspersed with the technical information to illustrate the use of each feature.

Tutorial: Description of the Umbrella Problem
Zoe doesn't like carrying her umbrella. It's bulky. She often leaves it behind, which forces her to continually buy new umbrellas. She hates getting caught in the rain without an umbrella, so each night she listens to the weather report to hear the probability estimate of whether it's going to rain the next day.

This guide employs several notational conventions. Many of DPL's features are accessed with a mouse. To *select* a menu item or icon from the tool bar means to position the arrow with the mouse over the program item of interest, and then to press the left mouse button once. Specific keys are identified in this guide by enclosing the name in double-guillemots, such as the enter key, «enter», and the backspace key, «backspace». Specific keystrokes to type are identified in quotation marks, so that the instruction to type plus forty would appear as "+40". Do not type the quotation marks.

DPL uses slightly different names for the decision elements than are employed in this book. Both this book and DPL use the term decision. DPL uses the term chance for an uncertain event, and value for an objective. DPL refers to the representation of any decision element generically as a node, whether it is a decision, uncertain event, or objective. DPL refers to the various branches associated with a decision (its alternatives) or an uncertain event (its possible outcomes) generically as states.

SPECIFYING DECISIONS

To specify a decision, select the yellow rectangular icon from the tool bar. A set of cross-hairs will appear on the screen. Position the cross-hairs at the location in the drawing pad where the decision element is to appear and press the left mouse button.[12] DPL subsequently asks for information about the decision. Enter the name of the decision in the space provided in the decision name dialogue box and select «OK». DPL next asks for the alternative names. The decision states dialogue box offers the default alternatives of yes and no. To accept the default state names, select «OK». Otherwise, enter each name of an alternative on a separate line. When finished, select «OK» to return to the influence diagram.

---

[12]As of the writing of this book, DPL uses a point-and-click procedure as opposed to the more recent Windows standard of drag-and-drop. The makers of DPL plan to eventually implement a drag-and-drop interface.

Tutorial: Specifying a Decision

To specify Zoe's primary decision, whether to take her umbrella or not, select the yellow rectangular icon, position the cross-hairs somewhere in the left side of the drawing pad, and select the location. Type the node name "Umbrella?" in the name dialogue box and select «OK». Select «OK» to accept the default alternatives in the states dialogue box. The following node will appear in the drawing pad:

```
┌─────────────┐
│             │
│  Umbrella?  │
│             │
└─────────────┘
```

SPECIFYING UNCERTAIN EVENTS

To specify an uncertain event, select the green elliptical icon from the tool bar. A set of cross-hairs will appear on the screen. Position the cross-hairs at the location in the drawing pad where the uncertain event is to appear and press the left mouse button. DPL subsequently asks for information about the uncertain event. Enter the name of the uncertain event in the space provided in the chance name dialogue box and select «OK». DPL next asks for the names of the possible outcomes. The chance states dialogue box offers the default outcomes of low, nominal, and high. To accept these default states, select «OK». Otherwise, enter the names of different possible outcomes, one per line.   When finished, select «OK» to return to the influence diagram.

Tutorial: Specifying an Uncertain Event

To specify Zoe's primary uncertain event, whether it rains or not, select the green elliptical icon, position the cross-hairs to the right and slightly above the decision node already included in the diagram, and select the location. Type the node name "Rain?" in the name dialogue box and select «OK». Type «backspace» to erase the default outcomes and type "rain «enter» sunshine", and then select «OK». The following node will appear in the drawing pad:

```
   ╭────────╮
   │  Rain? │
   ╰────────╯
```

```
┌─────────────┐
│             │
│  Umbrella?  │
│             │
└─────────────┘
```

SPECIFYING OBJECTIVES

To specify an objective, select the light-blue rectangular icon with rounded corners from the tool bar. A set of cross-hairs will appear on the screen. Position the cross-hairs at the location in the drawing pad where the uncertain event is to appear and select the location. DPL subsequently prompts for the name of the objective. Enter the name in the space provided in the value name dialogue box and select «OK».

Tutorial: Specifying Objectives
To specify Zoe's first objective, avoiding a catastrophe, select the light-blue rectangular icon with rounded corners, position the cross-hairs to the right of the uncertain event and at the same height as the decision node, and select the location. Type the node name "Catastrophe" in the name dialogue box and select «OK». The following node will appear in the drawing pad:

Create Zoe's additional objective, convenience, just under the catastrophe objective and total satisfaction to the right of the other objectives, following the same procedure.

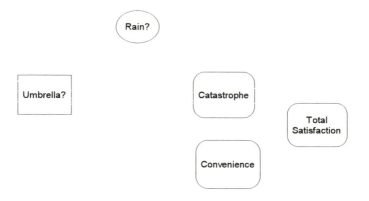

SPECIFYING INFLUENCES

To specify that one node influences another, select the influence arrow icon from the tool bar. Then select the node that is doing the influencing. Lastly, select the node that is being influenced. DPL responds by creating an arrow connecting the two.

Tutorial: Specifying Influence

To specify that the decision to bring an umbrella influences whether a catastrophe occurs, first select the influence arrow from the tool bar. Next select the decision node "Umbrella?" Lastly, select the value node "Catastrophe." The following relationship will appear in the drawing pad:

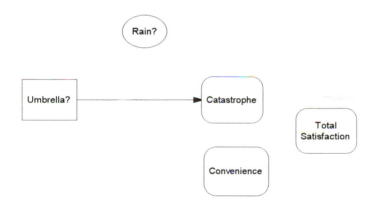

Following the same procedure, specify that the decision influences convenience, that whether it rains influences the occurrence of a catastrophe, and that both catastrophe and convenience influence total satisfaction.

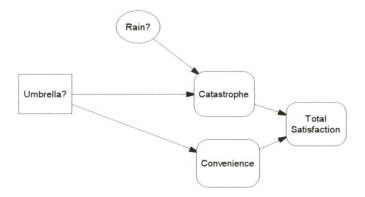

SPECIFYING VALUES

The DPL toolbar contains three data entry icons that appear when a node is selected. Whenever a node (or influence arrow) is selected it appears in purple. Each data entry icon displays a picture of a round green node with three branches stemming from it, with distinctive red highlighting indicating the icon's function. The first icon has red highlighting above the node. This is the *node name* icon. Selecting this icon calls up the name dialogue box and allows the user to revise the name of a node.

The second icon has red highlighting above each of the branches. This is the *node states* icon. Selecting this icon calls up the states dialogue box and allows the user to revise the state names. This icon can be used to add or delete states associated with a node. This icon does not appear when an objective node is selected, because there are no branches associated with an objective.

The third icon has red highlighting below each of the branches. This is the *node value* icon. This icon allows the user to specify the probabilities associated with an uncertain event and the payoffs associated with any type of node. For the analyses in this book, it is recommended that payoffs only be specified for objective nodes.

To specify the probabilities associated with an uncertain event, select the uncertain event; the event will appear in purple. Then select the node values icon. This calls up a value entry screen. This screen presents a decision tree indicating all possible outcomes and highlights the first possible outcome. Enter the probability of the first outcome at the top of the screen in the data entry area marked "probability." Then move to another possible outcome by selecting its location in the decision tree or by pressing «enter» twice. To return to the influence diagram, select «OK».

DPL also provides a wheel-of-fortune interface for entering probabilities. This feature can be extremely useful for eliciting probabilities from a decision maker. The wheel-of-fortune can be accessed from the node values entry screen of an uncertain event by selecting the «view» item from the menu and the «wheel» item from the submenu. DPL displays a pie chart with a colored section corresponding to the probability of each possible outcome associated with the uncertain event. Adjust any of the lines delimiting the areas by placing the cursor over a line, pressing and holding down the left-mouse button, and moving the mouse to move the line in the pie chart (this procedure for adjusting the lines is called *drag-and-drop*.) Once satisfied with the pie chart, select «OK». DPL will present a decision tree indicating the probability associated with each state as implied by the wheel of fortune.

To specify the payoffs associated with an objective, other than a total satisfaction objective, select the node and then select the node values icon. DPL displays a decision tree indicating all possible outcomes leading to the objective node. Enter a value associated with the first possible outcome. To move between states, either select a new state with the mouse, use the «up» and «down» arrows, or use the «enter» key. To return to the influence diagram, select «OK».

To specify the formula associated with a total satisfaction node, select the node and then select the node values icon. This calls up a data entry dialogue box. Type the formula for total satisfaction, as a function of the various objectives in the decision problem, in this box.

The name of each objective must be spelled exactly as DPL has represented it in its internal memory. This spelling can differ from the spelling of the node name in the influence diagram. In particular, DPL substitutes the underscore (_) for a blank space. Therefore, it is safest to avoid typing the names of objectives directly. Instead, select the «variable» button in the dialogue box to access a list of all the objectives, spelled according to DPL's internal name. To enter an objective into the total satisfaction formula, select the objective name, and select «OK». When done typing the formula for total satisfaction, select «OK» to return to the influence diagram.

Tutorial: Specifying Values

To specify the probability of rain, select the "Rain?" node and then select the node value icon. Enter the value ".4" in the box marked probability, to indicate that the probability of rain is 40%. Probability values must be specified as a value between 0 and 1.0. To enter a value as a percentage, type the number followed by the expression for divided by one hundred (/100), such as 40/100. Do not use the percentage sign (%). DPL will not recognize it.

Next, leave the second branch blank and select «OK». DPL will calculate that the correct probability of sunshine is 60% when it solves the problem.

To specify the payoffs associated with each possible outcome according to the objective, catastrophe, select the "Catastrophe" node and then select the node values icon. Type "100", then «enter» to enter the value one hundred on the first branch and move to the second branch. Enter one hundred on the second branch, zero on the third, and one hundred on the fourth. This payoff structure indicates that a catastrophe occurs only if Zoe does not bring her umbrella and it rains. Select «OK» to return to the influence diagram.

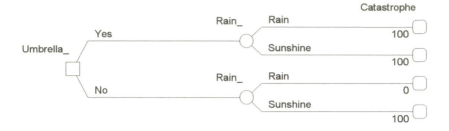

Similarly, specify that the payoff associated with convenience is zero when Zoe brings her umbrella and one hundred when she does not, which indicates that not bringing an umbrella maximizes her convenience:

To specify the formula for total satisfaction, select the "Total Satisfaction" node and then select the node values icon. Type the value ".80" followed by the asterisk (*) to indicate multiplication. Select the «variable» button in the dialogue box, select the word "Catastrophe" from the list of objectives, and then select «OK». Then type the expression "+.20*" and select the name "Convenience" from the list of objectives. The following formula indicates that avoiding a catastrophe is four times more important than convenience to Zoe:

$$.80*Catastrophe + .20*Convenience$$

RUNNING A DECISION ANALYSIS

To run a decision analysis select «Run» from the DPL menu and then select «Decision Analysis» from the submenu. DPL may subsequently prompt for various run-time features. Selecting «OK» in each dialogue box asks DPL to run the analysis using the default values for each of these.

DPL calculates the alternative with the highest payoff. The program first returns a dialogue box that indicates the payoff of the best alternative. Selecting «OK» brings up the next output screen, a decision tree indicating each alternative and the expected payoff associated with each. The best alternative is indicated with a bold line. DPL provides one additional screen, entitled DPL distributions. The interpretation of this screen, the DPL distribution, is beyond the scope of this book.

DPL has two primary display modes, corresponding to the influence diagram and decision tree representations of a decision problem. This book does not cover the use of DPL for specifying a decision tree. After running a decision analysis, DPL shifts from influence diagram to decision tree mode. To return to the original influence diagram press «tab».

Tutorial: Running a Decision Analysis
Running Zoe's decision analysis yields the following result:

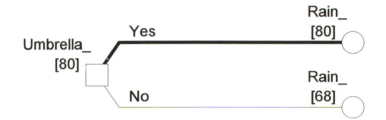

Zoe's best choice, under the circumstances, is to bring her umbrella. Her expected total satisfaction score is 80 out of a possible 100.

WINDOW MANAGEMENT

DPL employs standard windows management functions. To save a file, select «File» from the menu and «save» from the submenu. A dialogue box asks for the name for the file. DPL files use the .inf extension at the end of each file name to indicate that it contains an influence diagram. To open a previously saved file, select «File» from the menu and «open» from the submenu. A dialogue box asks for the name of the file. To print a screen, select «File» and then «Print Diagram». Most DPL screens can be printed.

DPL provides a scroll bar at the bottom and right sides of the drawing pad. Selecting the «left arrow» moves the viewer to the left side of the influence diagram. Similarly, the «right», «up» and «down» arrows move the viewer to different portions of the influence diagram. These features can be very useful when working with large influence diagrams.

DPL also allows the user to change the size of the decision elements so that more or less of the influence diagram appears on the screen. Selecting «View» and then «Zoom In» from the menu makes the diagram larger and easier to read. Selecting «View» and then «Zoom Out» makes the diagram smaller, allowing more of the diagram to appear on the screen at one time. Selecting «View» and then «Zoom Full» makes the diagram exactly fill the entire screen.

Nodes within a diagram can be rearranged at any time. To move a node, first select it. Then press the left mouse button twice, in rapid succession. A set of cross-hairs will appear. (If the cross-hairs do not appear, try again. They will not come up if the time between mouse clicks is too long.) Move the cross-hairs to the desired location and press the left mouse button again. To delete a node, select the node and then press the «delete» key.

To undo a previous command, select «Edit» and then «Undo» from the menu.

SENSITIVITY ANALYSIS

Sensitivity analysis identifies how the best alternative changes with minor modifications to the influence diagram. In particular, it is often useful to know how the decision changes as the value for a probability, objective score, or tradeoff weight varies. Performing a sensitivity analysis for single value (called a parameter) requires three steps in DPL.

Define parameter. Create an objective node with the name of the parameter in the upper left-hand corner of the influence diagram. Specify an initial value for this node equal to the value used in previous calculations. This node should not have any influence arrows entering or leaving it.

Specify parameter's influence. Select a node that employs the parameter and select the node values icon. Replace the current number with the name of the parameter from the list of objectives. Repeat if there is more than one node that uses the parameter.

Run sensitivity analysis. Select the «Run» feature from the pull-down menu and the «Value Sensitivity Analysis (Rainbow Diagram)» from the submenu. DPL will present a sensitivity options dialogue box. Select the parameter for the sensitivity analysis from the list of objective nodes provided. Next press the left mouse button twice, in rapid succession. The nominal value for the parameter will appear in the dialogue box. Enter the minimum and maximum values to be used in the sensitivity analysis. Then skip to the bottom of the dialogue box and enter 21 as the number of values to include in the analysis. Select «OK» to run the analysis.

Tutorial: Sensitivity Analysis
To identify the smallest probability of rain for which Zoe should take her umbrella, run a sensitivity analysis. First, specify that the probability of rain is a parameter by creating an objective node in the upper left-hand corner of the influence diagram, as illustrated below:

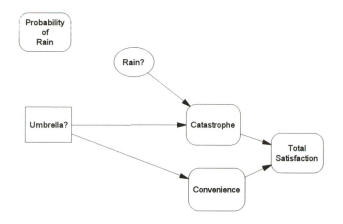

Next select the "Rain?" node to highlight it, and select the node values icon to see the current probability of rain (.40). Enter the name of the parameter "Probability_of_Rain" to indicate where the parameter value for the probability of rain is stored. Leave the probability on the bottom branch unspecified. If the last branch of the uncertain event is specified, DPL will respond with an error message during the sensitivity analysis calculation.

Lastly, select «Run» from the menu and «Value Sensitivity Analysis (Rainbow Diagram)» from the submenu. DPL responds with the sensitivity options dialogue box. Select the name «Probability_of_Rain» from the list at the top of the dialogue box and then double-click the mouse to specify the nominal value of the parameter. Specify 0 as the starting value, 1 as the ending value, and that DPL should include 21 values in its sensitivity analysis. DPL will provide the following graph:

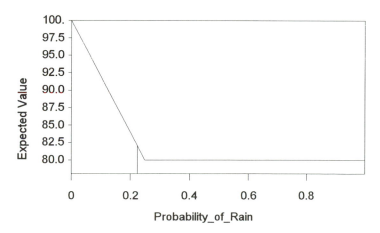

The output indicates that if the probability of rain is greater than about 25%, Zoe should take her umbrella. If the probability is less, then she should not bring her umbrella.

EXPECTED VALUE OF PERFECT INFORMATION

The expected payoff to a decision problem can always be improved by knowing what the outcome to an uncertain event would be, in advance of making a decision. DPL can indicate precisely how much. To change a risky decision problem into a perfect information problem, delete any arrows from the decision node to the uncertain event, draw an arrow from the uncertain event to the decision node, and rerun the analysis.

Tutorial: Expected Value of Perfect Information

Perform an EVPI analysis to identify whether Zoe should wait until the morning, when she's about to leave, to obtain an accurate weather report that will indicate with certainty whether it is raining. Clearly, if it is raining she would bring her umbrella. To calculate how much her expected satisfaction would improve by obtaining this additional information, draw an influence arrow from the uncertain event, rain, to the primary decision, as illustrated below, and rerun the decision analysis.

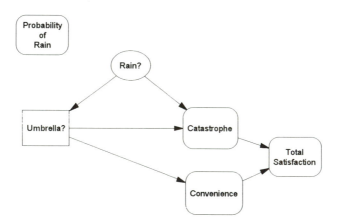

DPL will provide the following solution:

The solution indicates that if it rains, Zoe should take her umbrella, and that her total satisfaction in this case would be 80. If it does not rain, she should not take her umbrella, and her total satisfaction is 100. Because she does not know whether it is going to rain, her expected satisfaction is 92.

The solution to the risky problem suggested that Zoe take her umbrella, just in case it rains, which led to an expected satisfaction of 80. By knowing, at the time of her decision, whether it is raining, her expected total satisfaction increased by 12 points. So, if it is not too much of a bother, Zoe should listen to the weather report before she leaves.

❏ FOR ADDITIONAL INFORMATION ON

Using DPL:

ADA Decision Systems. 1995. *DPL Standard Version User Guide,* Student Edition. Belmont, CA: Duxbury Press.

Appendix B
USING A SPREADSHEET
FOR DECISION ANALYSIS

OBJECTIVES
After studying this appendix you should be able to

■ create a decision tree using a spreadsheet,

■ create a scorecard using a spreadsheet.

Spreadsheet programs are highly flexible and widely available. Some popular spreadsheets are Lotus 1-2-3, Excel, and Quattro Pro. It is assumed that the reader has used a spreadsheet before. It does not matter which one, because the basic features in all spreadsheets are about the same.

This appendix describes how to create a decision tree and a scorecard with a spreadsheet. A tutorial example is interspersed with the technical information to illustrate the procedures.

For large decision problems with numerous alternatives and uncertain events, spreadsheets can be very cumbersome. However, for smaller problems, the use of a spreadsheet can be quite convenient. Additionally, spreadsheets are useful for creating scorecards, which are excellent presentation tools. (Scorecards are discussed in Chapter Five.) Moreover, spreadsheets are particularly convenient for solving decision problems with multiple objectives and no uncertain events.

A spreadsheet contains a rectangular grid. Each cell in the grid can contain a different number. Most importantly, a cell can contain a formula to calculate a number using the numbers contained in other cells. Popular spreadsheets generally label the columns with successive letters of the alphabet and rows with numbers. An individual cell is identified by the letter associated with the column in which it is located followed by the number associated with its row. For example, cell A2 is located in the first column, two rows down.

	A	B	C	D	E	. . .
1					E1	
2	A2					
3				D3		
4						
. . .						

CREATING A DECISION TREE

This book follows the convention that time runs from the top of a spreadsheet downward. The first row represents the current moment. Thus, for most decision problems, the first row includes a list of the alternatives to the primary decision. Each alternative is placed in a separate cell.

Tutorial Example: The Primary Decision

This appendix uses the same tutorial presented in Appendix A, Zoe's decision whether to take an umbrella. The first step is to enter the primary decision. Enter the name of the primary decision in the first column and each of the alternatives in subsequent cells in the first row. Leave some blank columns between entries to anticipate branching. In general, the more uncertain events and subsequent decisions in a problem, the more space will be needed between alternatives of the primary decision. Should the amount of space initially allocated prove to be too small, additional columns can be inserted into the spreadsheet as the analysis proceeds.

	A	B	C	D
1	Umbrella?	Yes		No
2				
3				
4				

Subsequent decisions and uncertain events are placed on successive lines. The names of the branches associated with each successive decision element must be repeated underneath each of the branches from the preceding element. Each decision is placed in its own row. Uncertain events require two rows. The first row identifies the names of each possible outcome. The second row identifies the probability of each possible outcome.

Tutorial Example: A Subsequent Uncertain Event
To specify the uncertain event of whether or not it rains, type the possible outcomes "rain" and "sun" in row 2 and the probabilities associated with each in row 3 as follows:

	A	B	C	D	E
1	Umbrella?	Yes		No	
2	Rain?	Rain	Sun	Rain	Sun
3	Pr[Rain]	.4	.6	.4	.6
4					

Once all of the decisions and uncertain events have been represented on the spreadsheet, the first phase of creating a decision tree is finished. A scorecard is used to complete the decision tree.

CREATING A SCORECARD

A scorecard indicates how each final outcome compares according to the objectives included in the analysis. The final outcomes are indicated by the individual branches identified after all decisions and uncertain events have been represented in the decision tree. For decision problems that include only one decision and do not include any uncertain events, the final outcomes are the same as the alternatives associated with the primary decision.

To create a scorecard, the objectives for the decision problem are represented in successive rows at the bottom of the decision tree. Each cell entry indicates how the branch, identified by the column in the spreadsheet, scores on the objective identified by the row.

Tutorial Example: Creating a Scorecard
To create a scorecard for Zoe's decision, enter her two objectives, avoiding catastrophe and convenience, and the scores associated with each outcome in the last rows of the spreadsheet, as follows:

	A	B	C	D	E
1	Umbrella?	Yes		No	
2	Rain?	Rain	Sun	Rain	Sun
3	Pr[Rain]	.4	.6	.4	.6
4	Catastrophe	100	100	0	100
5	Convenience	0	0	100	100

EVALUATING A SCORECARD

To solve a decision problem represented as a scorecard involves calculating the value for "Total Satisfaction" using tradeoff weights. The tradeoff weights associated with each objective are placed down the right side of the spreadsheet. These weights are then multiplied by the entries in each successive column to identify the desirability of each final outcome. The total satisfaction of each possible outcome is recorded at the bottom of the decision tree.

Next, the expected value of each alternative is calculated as the weighted average across each final outcome associated with an alternative. The weight of each final outcome is the probability that it occurs if the alternative is selected. Determining this probability can be complicated for problems with several uncertain events and especially complicated for problems with more than one decision.

Tutorial Example: Evaluating a Scorecard
To evaluate Zoe's scorecard, enter her tradeoff weights of .80 for catastrophe and .2 for convenience in column F, lines 4 and 5. Calculate the desirability of the final outcome in column A, which occurs if Zoe takes her umbrella and it rains, by entering the following formula in cell B6:

$$\$F4*B4 + \$F5*B5$$

Copy this formula into cells C6 though E6. The dollar signs in the formula specify that when copied to another cell, the item will be multiplied by the cell entry in column F. For example, in C6 the formula will appear as follows:

$$\$F4*C4 + \$F5*C5$$

This formula provides the weighted average for total satisfaction in the case of the second possible outcome. At this point, the spreadsheet should look like the following:

	A	B	C	D	E	F
1	Umbrella?	Yes		No		
2	Rain?	Rain	Sun	Rain	Sun	Tradeoff Weights
3	Pr[Rain]	.4	.6	.4	.6	
4	Catastrophe	100	100	0	100	.80
5	Convenience	0	0	100	100	.20
6	Total Satisfaction	80	80	20	100	

Lastly, calculate the desirability of each alternative by multiplying the total satisfaction associated with each possible outcome (row 6) by the probability of each possible outcome (row 3). Type the following formula in cell B7:

$$B6*B3 + C6*C3$$

Copy this formula into cell D6. The final spreadsheet should look like the following:

	A	B	C	D	E	F
1	Umbrella?	Yes		No		
2	Rain?	Rain	Sun	Rain	Sun	Tradeoff Weights
3	Pr[Rain]	.4	.6	.4	.6	
4	Catastrophe	100	100	0	100	.80
5	Convenience	0	0	100	100	.20
6	Total Satisfaction	80	80	20	100	
7		80		68		

According to this analysis, Zoe should take her umbrella.

Appendix C
PROBABILITY REVIEW

OBJECTIVES
After studying this appendix you should be able to

- draw a Venn diagram to illustrate the interrelationship between the probabilities of events,
- apply the principles of probability to decision analysis.

This appendix reviews essential probability concepts employed in the analysis of decision problems.

PROBABILITY OF AN EVENT

The concept of probability can be well illustrated with a Venn diagram. The total diagram represents the universe of all possible outcomes. The area enclosed in a shape represents those possible outcomes corresponding to an event under consideration. Thus, the probability of an event, denoted Pr[*event*], is proportional to the area enclosed; the more area, the more likely the event.

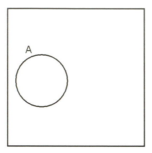

A sure event that will definitely occur is represented by a figure that consumes 100% of the Venn diagram. An impossible event that will definitely not occur is represented by a single point that consumes 0% of the Venn diagram. These represent the extreme values for the probability of an event. The likelihood of any event must be between 0% and 100%.

Probability of an Event: Relations between the U. S. and Cuba, Part I
Juan, an entrepreneur from the Dominican Republic, is considering whether to produce premium quality cigars for export to the United States. Cuba has a longstanding reputation for producing the best cigars. However, given the uneasy relationship between the United States and Cuba, importation of cigars from Cuba has been banned. Should relations between the two countries improve within the next five years, the profitability of Juan's enterprise would be affected.

Consequently, Juan included as an uncertain event in his decision analysis that the United States and Cuba become allies. Juan reasoned that one of three possibilities seemed plausible: (A) The countries could become allies, (B) The two countries could go to war with each other, or (C) The uneasy relationship could continue.

He decided that the probability of an alliance, Pr[A], is about 20%. The Venn diagram above illustrates his probability, where A equals the event that Cuba and United States become allies within five years.

The diagram represents Juan's personal assessment of the likelihood of the event that Cuba and the United States become allies within five years. It is his opinion. Probabilities that represent an individual's opinion about the likelihood of an event are referred to as subjective probabilities. Other individuals may hold a different opinion about the likelihood of the same event.

COMPLEMENT OF AN EVENT

The *complement* of an event includes all possible outcomes in which an event does not occur. The complement is thus an event itself and is denoted as the name of the event followed by a single quotation mark. For example, A′ (pronounced "A complement" or "A prime") represents the event that A does not occur. Either an event occurs or it does not. Therefore, an event and its complement exhaust the range of all possibilities, as illustrated in the following Venn diagram:

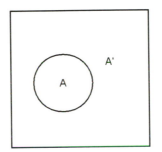

Moreover, the following mathematical relationship holds:

$$Pr[A] + Pr[A'] = 100\%$$

Solving this equation for the probability of the complement yields the following important relationship:

$$Pr[A'] = 100\% - Pr[A]$$

Complement of an Event: Relations between the U. S. and Cuba, Part II
Juan's venture into the cigar business has its best chances if Cuba and the United States do not become allies. The probability of this event is equal to the complement of their becoming allies, and is calculated as follows:

$$Pr[A'] = 100\% - Pr[A]$$

$$= 100\% - 20\%$$

$$= 80\%$$

INTERSECTION

The probability that two events both occur is called their *intersection*, which is written A∧B. The relationship between two events can be depicted in a Venn diagram with two overlapping shapes, as illustrated below:

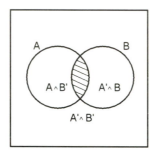

The shaded area indicates the intersection of events A and B. The larger the intersection, the more likely both A and B will occur. The probability of the intersection of two events can never be greater than the probability of either event. Unless A and B represent the same event, there will be outcomes in which either A occurs and B does not, B occurs and A does not, or both. The area of A not included in the intersection in the Venn diagram above represents the occurrence of event A but not B, A∧B′. The area of B not included in the intersection represents the occurrence of event B but not event A, A′∧B. The area outside of the two shapes represents the occurrence of neither event A nor event B, A′∧B′.

MUTUAL EXCLUSIVITY

Two events are *mutually exclusive* if the probability of both occurring is impossible. This relationship can be illustrated by a Venn diagram of two events with no area in common as follows:

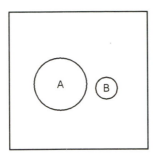

Being mutually exclusive does not mean that two events are unrelated. To the contrary, mutual exclusivity is a very special kind of relationship. Knowing that one of the events occurred indicates that the other event did not occur. In this sense, the two events can be viewed as competing with each other. One example of mutually exclusive events is an event A and its complement A'. An event and its complement cannot both occur.

Mutual Exclusivity: Relations between the U. S. and Cuba, Part III
Juan felt that the probability of the United States and Cuba going to war has a remote probability of about 10%. Importantly, the two countries cannot both go to war and be allies. These two events are mutually exclusive and can be represented by the Venn diagram above with event A equal to the event that the U. S. and Cuba become allies, and event B equal to the event that the U. S. and Cuba go to war.

CONDITIONAL PROBABILITY

A *conditional probability*–denoted Pr[A|B], and read as "the probability of A given B"–is the probability that an uncertain event occurs assuming that another uncertain event has already occurred. The event B is referred to as the conditioning event. This concept is particularly useful when evaluating sequences of uncertain events.

To identify Pr[A|B], the analyst must imagine that event B has already occurred and then identify the probability of A based on this new point of reference. In essence, this involves revising the universe of all possible outcomes as follows:

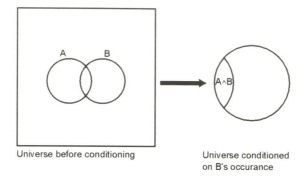

Universe before conditioning   Universe conditioned
                                             on B's occurance

The probability of A in the original, unconditioned universe, is the portion of the Venn diagram enclosed by the shape marked A. In the conditional universe, all possible outcomes in which B does not occur (B′) are eliminated. The probability of A occurring, in the conditioned universe, is the portion of outcomes in which B occurs that A also occurs, A∧B. Following this logic leads to a formula for the conditional probability of A|B:

$$\Pr[A|B] \; = \; \frac{\Pr[A\wedge B]}{\Pr[B]}$$

Conditional Probability: Relations between the U. S. and Cuba, Part IV
An important event associated with whether the United States and Cuba develop an alliance is whether Cuba institutes a democratic form of governance. Juan created the following Venn diagram to illustrate the relationship between the two events:

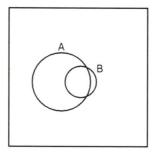

Where,

A = Cuba and the United States become allies within five years

B = Cuba institutes a democratic government within five years

His subjective estimates for the probabilities illustrated in the diagram are as follows:

$Pr[A] = 20\%$

$Pr[B] = 40\%$

$Pr[A \wedge B] = 15\%$

The conditional probability of Cuba and the United States becoming allies if Cuba institutes a democratic government can be calculated as follows from the given information:

$$Pr[A|B] = \frac{Pr[A \wedge B]}{Pr[B]}$$

$$Pr[A|B] = \frac{15\%}{20\%}$$

$$Pr[A|B] = 75\%$$

This analysis indicates that if Cuba institutes a democratic government, the probability of an alliance is very strong. This probabilistic relationship is illustrated in the Venn diagram by the area associated with event A overlapping a particularly large portion of event B.

INDEPENDENCE

An event A is *independent* or unrelated to another event B, if knowing the outcome of event B does not provide any information about the outcome of event A. Mathematically, this is expressed as the equivalence between the probability of event A and the conditional probability of event A given event B has occurred:

$$Pr[A] = Pr[A|B]$$

This relationship is quite different from mutual exclusivity in which there is no intersection between events A and B. The independence of two events implies there is a very specific, nonzero intersection between the two events. This amount can be determined by substituting the formula for conditional probability into the above definition of independence:

$$Pr[A] = \frac{Pr[A \wedge B]}{Pr[B]}$$

$$\rightarrow \quad Pr[A \wedge B] = Pr[A] \times Pr[B]$$

Independence: Relations between the U. S. and Cuba, Part V

A relatively unimportant event associated with whether the United States and Cuba develop an alliance is whether Cuba wins the gold medal for soccer at the Olympic games. Juan estimates that the Cuban soccer team has a 30% chance of winning the gold medal. Since the two events are independent, the probability of both event A, a Cuba-U.S. alliance, and event B, a gold medal in soccer, can be calculated as follows:

$$Pr[A \wedge B] = Pr[A] \times Pr[B]$$

$$Pr[A \wedge B] = 20\% \times 30\%$$

$$Pr[A \wedge B] = 6\%$$

This relationship is illustrated by the following Venn diagram:

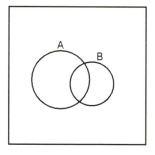

Where,
A = Cuba and the United States become allies within five years
B = Cuba wins the Olympic gold medal in soccer

TOTAL PROBABILITY

The *total probability* of an event expresses the probability of an event, A, as a function of a preceding event, B, when the outcome of B is not yet known. The precedence of one event to another is illustrated by the following influence diagram:

Certainly, the probability of event A can be simply represented as Pr[A]. However, in some circumstances it is advantageous to define the probability of A in terms of the various possibilities associated with a preceding event, B. The occurrence of A can be defined conditionally on B according to the following decision tree:

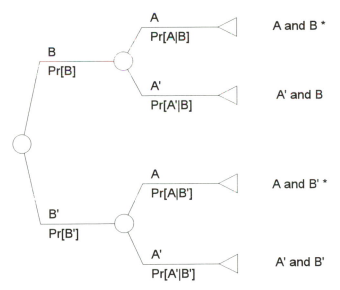

* These two final outcomes comprise the occurrence of event A.

This tree indicates that event A can occur in one of two ways; either after event B occurs, or after event B does not occur. Mathematically, this relationship is written as follows:

$$Pr[A] = Pr[A \wedge B] + Pr[A \wedge B']$$

This formula can be expanded using the following important relationship which derives from the formula for conditional probability:

$$Pr[A|B] = \frac{Pr[A \wedge B]}{Pr[B]}$$

$$\rightarrow \quad Pr[A \wedge B] = Pr[A|B] \times Pr[B]$$

This formula indicates that the probability that both events A and B occur can be calculated as the series of steps along the top path in the decision tree ending at $A \wedge B$. The first step is that B occurs and has an associated probability $Pr[B]$. The second step is that A occurs, given that B has already occurred and has an associated probability $Pr[A|B]$. The probability of these events happening in succession is the product of their probabilities, $Pr[A|B] \times Pr[B]$. Substituting this formula into the formula for total probability yields the following:

$$Pr[A] = Pr[A|B] \times Pr[B] + Pr[A|B'] \times Pr[A|B']$$

This formula is used in the decomposition approach to assessing the probability of an event (presented in Chapter Four) for situations in which the occurrence of the event of interest is intricately associated with the occurrence of another event.

BAYES' THEOREM

Bayes' theorem is a procedure for updating one's estimate for the probability of an event in light of new information. This formula has wide applicability. Its usefulness is particularly recognizable in the field of medicine, where the results of a test could further suggest that a patient has a specific condition, and in criminal investigations where additional information can further suggest who committed a crime.

The presentation in this section assumes Bayes' theorem is being used to diagnose whether a particular condition (event A) exists, and that a test will be performed to help with the diagnosis. A positive result from the test is designated as event B. The probability of the condition prior to receipt of additional information is denoted as $Pr[A]$, and is referred to as the *prior probability*.

Subsequently, new information is obtained that should help distinguish whether the condition exists. The likelihood of observing this information, such as a positive result on a medical test, given that the condition exists is denoted as $Pr[B|A]$. However, there is also a possibility of a *false positive*, a positive result on the test given that the condition does not exist, which is denoted as Pr[B|A′]. Similarly, a test result can come back negative even if the condition exists. This event is known as a *false negative* and is denoted Pr[B′|A].

The following decision tree summarizes the possible combinations of events:

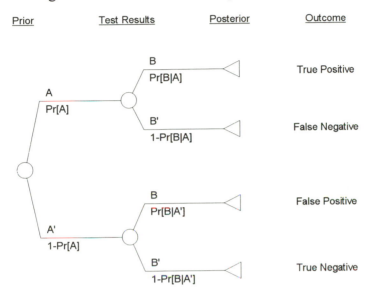

The diagram indicates that a positive test result can occur under one of two circumstances: a true positive or a false positive. According to the formula for conditional probability, the probability of the event given that a positive test result occurred, known as the *posterior probability*, is obtained using the formula for conditional probability, as follows:

$$Pr[A|B] = \frac{Pr[A \wedge B]}{Pr[B]}$$

Using the formula for total probability yields the following formula with an expanded denominator. The terms in the denominator correspond to two branches of the decision tree above in which a positive test result occurs:

$$Pr[A|B] = \frac{Pr[A \wedge B]}{Pr[A \wedge B] + Pr[A \wedge B']}$$

Substituting the formula Pr[A∧B]=Pr[B|A] × Pr[A] for each of the three terms in the formula leads to the final form, known as Bayes' theorem.

$$\Pr[A|B] \ = \ \frac{\Pr[B|A] \times \Pr[A]}{\Pr[B|A] \times \Pr[A] \ + \ \Pr[B|A\,'] \times \Pr[A\,']}$$

Bayes' Theorem: A Test for HIV

Sonya Dawes came to Dr. Raisa Miller complaining of a cold that would not go away, and a persistent rash. Dr. Miller suspected that Sonya might have contracted the HIV virus, the virus that causes AIDS. About one in every five patients Dr. Miller had seen with similar symptoms turned out to be HIV-positive. So Dr. Miller identified her initial estimate of the probability for the Event A, that Sonya was HIV-positive, as $\Pr[A]=20\%$. To be more certain, she ordered a blood test.

The particular blood that was available at the time was not perfect, which is typical of many types of diagnostic tests. The test does not exactly identify whether an individual is HIV-positive. The way these tests work, the test reports either a positive or a negative result. The event that the test comes back positive can be called Event B. If the individual is HIV-positive, then the test will most likely return a positive result. This particular test comes back positive 99% of the time when the patient has the virus: $\Pr[B|A] = 99\%$. But this does not mean that there is a 99% chance that the patient is HIV-positive.

Sometimes, the blood test comes back positive when an individual does not have the virus. This occurrence is referred to as a false positive. This particular blood test returns a false positive 2% of the time when the patient does not have the virus: $\Pr[B|A'] = 2\%$. So if a test result comes back positive, it might be because the patient is HIV-positive or it might be a false positive as a result of chance. Moreover, even if the test comes back negative, it does not necessarily mean that the patient is HIV-negative. Sometimes, the blood test fails to return a positive indication for an HIV-positive blood sample, an occurrence known as a false negative. In fact, this particular blood test returns a false negative for one out of every one hundred HIV-positive blood samples analyzed: $\Pr[B'|A] = 1\%$, the complement of $\Pr[B|A]$.

Sonya's test result came back positive. Dr. Miller calculated the posterior probability that Sonya was HIV-positive using Bayes' theorem as follows:

$$\Pr[A|B] \ = \ \frac{.99 \times .20}{.99 \times .20 \ + \ .02 \times (1 - .20)}$$

$$= \frac{.198}{.198 \ + \ .016}$$

$$= .925$$

Based on this result, Dr. Miller was much more confident that Sonya might have the HIV virus. But she was not yet convinced enough. There was still a 7.5% probability that Sonya did not have the HIV virus. Because she was far from certain concerning Sonya's diagnosis, Dr. Miller informed Sonya that she strongly suspected the HIV virus, but that she needed to perform additional tests to be more certain.

It is this possibility of false positives and the anxiety they can produce that makes testing for HIV among the general population controversial and test counseling so important. The probability that a patient whose blood test returned positive has the HIV virus strongly depends on the prior probability, Pr[A]. It is estimated that about one in every 200 Americans carries the HIV virus. Thus, an individual chosen at random has a prior probability of HIV-positivity of about 0.5%. Using the blood test described above, only 20% of the people who test positive will actually have the HIV virus. (You can use Bayes' rule to double check this result.) Most importantly, four out of five people who test positive will go through the anxiety of thinking they might have the virus, even though they don't.

EXPECTED VALUE

The expected value [EV] of an uncertain event is the weighted average of the event's possible payoffs, where each payoff is weighted according to the probability of its occurrence, as algebraically represented below. The motivation for using the expected value is discussed in Chapter One-B, which covers the decision criterion of maximizing the expected monetary value.

$$EV[x] = \sum_{i=1}^{I} x_i \times Pr[x_i]$$

Where,
i = index of all possible outcomes
x_i = payoff associated with outcome i

Expected Value: Relations between the U. S. and Cuba, Part VI
Juan estimates that the profits on his cigar venture will be strongly affected by the continuing relationship between the United States and Cuba as follows:

Cuba-U.S. Relationship	Juan's Five-Year Profits	Probability
Alliance	-$5,000,000	20%
War	$2,000,000	10%
Uneasy Peace	$20,000,000	70%

The expected value of this venture can be calculated as follows:

EV[Juan's Cigars]=

-$5,000,000 × 20% + $2,000,000 × 10% + $20,000,000 × 70%

= $13,200,000

This profit represents an average across all possible circumstances, yet under no circumstance will Juan's profits exactly equal $13,200,000.

❏ EXERCISES

1. Kara manages a stock portfolio. Currently, she has a large investment in the auto industry. She is particularly worried about two risks that could hurt her investment: the event that auto sales will slump, and the event that the Federal Reserve raises interest rates. The probability of an auto sales slump is 30%, the probability of an interest rate increase is 50%, and the probability of both is 15%. Draw a Venn diagram to show the interrelationship between the probabilities of these two events. What is the probability that auto sales do not slump? What is the probability that auto sales do not slump but interest rates are increased? What is the probability of neither event occurring?

2. Mustafa has a lump on his chest. There is a 40% chance that it is cancerous. If it is cancerous, there is an 80% chance that it can be completely removed. Draw a decision tree to illustrate the sequence of events: that the lump is cancerous, and that it cannot be completely removed. What is the probability that Mustafa has a cancer that cannot be completely removed?

3. Treasure Hunters Enterprises is planning to search for the Olympiad, a merchant boat which sank in 1620. Their chance of finding the boat using new underwater search technology is 40%. It sank in very deep water. Their chance of recovering the boat, if found, is only 25%. Finally, the chance that there is any treasure aboard is 80%. Draw a decision tree to illustrate the sequence of events: finding the boat, recovering it, and finding treasure. What is the probability that they recover the boat? What is the probability that they recover the boat and find treasure? What is the probability that they find the boat but are unable to recover it? What is the probability that they don't even find the boat?

4. Leather Gears is a struggling shoe manufacturer. They recently hired PDQ Associates to help them turn their business around, providing them with a three-month contract. The probability that PDQ will be successful depends on whether they gain the cooperation of the department heads. If they do gain cooperation, then there is a 60% chance they can save the company. However, they might be able to save the company without cooperation, although there is only a 35% chance under such circumstances. The probability that they gain cooperation is 75%. What is the probability that PDQ Associates saves the company?

5. Twenty percent of the train authority's track workers would make good supervisors; 60% have good communication skills; 40% of employees have both good communication skills and would make good supervisors. Draw a Venn diagram to show the interrelationship between the probability that an employee has good communication skills and that the employee would make a good supervisor. What is the probability that an employee with good communication skills would make a good supervisor? What is the probability that an employee who does not have good communication skills would make a good supervisor?

6. Eighty-five percent of all new businesses fail within the first year; 92% fail within the first five years. What is the probability that a business survives the first year? What is the probability that a business survives its first five years? What is the probability that a business survives its first five years, given that it has already survived its first year?

Appendix D
TIME VALUE OF MONEY

OBJECTIVES
After studying this appendix you should be able to

- calculate how an investment grows over time,

- compare the desirability of payments for different amounts of money occurring at different times in the future,

- choose an appropriate interest rate for a decision problem.

Many decision problems involve the payment of money at some time in the future, as opposed to today. (The term *payment* in this appendix is used in its generic sense to indicate either the disbursement or receipt of money.) For example, a store owner may be faced with purchasing his building. This represents a choice between making a lot of smaller rent payments or one large purchase payment. This appendix describes how to compare such alternatives from the financial perspective. The key to evaluating such decision problems is understanding that money–which when discussing finance is called *capital*–can generate additional money through investments.

Time Value of Money: When Do You Want Your Money?
Which would you rather have: $10,000 right now or $10,000 one year from now? The correct answer is to take the money now, because $10,000 one year from now is not worth as much as it is today. The idea that the value of money differs depending on when the transaction occurs is known as the *time value of money*. How much is $10,000 next year worth? Well, if you could buy a one-year certificate of deposit (CD) at a bank for only $9,434 that is guaranteed to pay $10,000 next year then you might say it is worth $9,434 .

This appendix describes the process by which an investment grows over time. It is this process that provides the basis for comparing future payments that occur at different times to one another. The appendix then describes the technique for comparing future payments. The results of future value and net present value calculations are highly dependent on the interest rate used. However, interest rates vary greatly across decision makers and over time. The last section discusses how to identify an appropriate interest rate for use in a decision problem.

FUTURE VALUE

Money grows over time such that money invested today will be worth more in the future. In this regard, one can talk about the *future value* [FV] value of an investment–how much an investment will be worth in the future. The FV depends on the size of the original investment, the number of years of the investment, and the interest rate applied to it.

The following formula for the FV of an investment indicates how much it will be worth after one year. The formula is equally correct for other time periods such as a month or a day. However, for simplicity, in this appendix it will be assumed that all time periods are specified in years.

$$S_1 = S_0 + (S_0 \times i)$$

$$\rightarrow \quad S_1 = S_0 \times (1 + i)$$

Where,
S_1 = the size of the payment at the end of year
i = the interest rate
S_0 = the amount of money invested at the beginning of the year

At the end of one year, the amount of money in the account (S_1) is equal to the amount of original investment (S_0) plus accumulated interest which is calculated as a percentage of the investment ($S_0 \times i$). A larger initial investment or a higher interest rate each results in more money at the end of the year.

Future Value: Kelvin's Car Purchase, Part I
Kelvin is considering purchasing a car, either this year or next. He has saved $10,000 and wonders how much more he will have if he invests his money for one year at 6%. The one-year future value of this investment is $10,000 \times (1 + .06)$ or $10,600.

One can also increase the future value of an investment by leaving the money in the account for an additional year. In this way, the investment earns another year's interest and interest on the income earned in the previous year. The process of paying interest on interest already received is called *compounding the interest*. It is through this compounding of interest that investments left for many years grow to be quite sizable.

The formula for the FV of a two-year investment can be straightforwardly derived using the one-year formula twice. The value after the second year is equal to the accumulation on the amount after the first year, plus the income earned over the second year:

$$S_2 = S_1 \times (1 + i)$$

After the first year, the initial investment will have grown to $S_1 = [S_0 \times (1 + i)]$. This formula can be substituted into the equation above as follows:

$$S_2 = [S_0 \times (1 + i)] \times (1 + i)$$

$$\rightarrow \quad S_2 = S_0 \times (1 + i)^2$$

Future Value: Kelvin's Car Purchase, Part II

Kelvin was disappointed with the amount his money would accumulate after one year and decided to calculate how much his investment would grow by postponing his purchase for two years. By leaving his $10,600 investment in for a second year, the investment grows to $10,600 \times (1 + .06)$ or $11,236. In the second year, the investment earned $636 as opposed to the $600 in the first year, because the investment paid interest on the interest accumulated in the first year. (Note: He could also have calculated his FV after two years as $10,000 \times [1 + .06]^2$.)

The formula for the FV of an investment after more than two years can be derived from the single-period interest formula by repeatedly applying the procedure presented above for deriving the two-year interest rate. The end result is the following formula:

$$S_n = S_0 \times (1 + i)^n$$

Future Value: Saving for Retirement

Kwamee is concerned about having enough money when he retires so that he'll be able to travel. On the one hand, it will be easier to save money when he's older, because he'll be earning a larger salary and some of his major purchases will have been paid off. On the other hand, he knows that money invested today will grow substantially. To verify the impact of the compounding of interest, he calculated how much an investment of $10,000 today would grow to 30 years from now at 6%:

$$\$10,000 \times (1+.06)^{30} = \$57,435$$

As a result of the substantial compounding associated with saving money while he is still young, Kwamee decided it was important to start saving now.

NET PRESENT VALUE

One method conventionally used for evaluating a payment (or set of payments) that will occur in the future is to calculate how much money would have to be placed in the bank today to provide for the future payment (or payments). This important standard is known as the *net present value* [NPV] of a future payment. The formula for NPV can be straightforwardly derived by solving the FV formula for the initial investment, S_0 required to achieve S_n, as follows:

$$S_n = S_0 \times (1+i)^n$$

$$\rightarrow \quad S_0 = \frac{S_n}{(1+i)^n}$$

Net Present Value: Deferring a Student Loan
Shannon owes $10,000 on her student loan. She is currently a graduate student and is allowed to defer current payments. However, over the summer she earned $10,000 and is considering paying off her loan. Alternatively, she could wait until the end of next year to pay, or request a five-year deferment. She was wondering whether the financial savings of deferring payment was substantial enough to justify filing for deferment.

The NPV of a payment for $10,000 can be calculated as follows. Shannon used the interest rate of 6%, since that is what she currently earns in her bank account.

$$\$10,000/(1+.06)^1 = \$9,434$$

In this case, the NPV calculation effectively discounted the $10,000 payment to account for interest that could have accrued during the year. By deferring payment for one year, she effectively reduced the size of the payment by $566.

The calculation for a five-year deferment is similar:

$$\$10,000 / (1 + .06)^5 = \$7,473$$

Payments which occur further into the future are worth less than similar payments occurring sooner. In this case, the difference between two payments of $10,000 occurring four years apart was an NPV close to $2,000. In other words, by deferring payment the additional four years, Shannon saves $2,000.

Shannon decided that the five-year deferment was clearly worthwhile, and she invested her summer earnings in the bank.

Quite often, decision problems involve evaluating a series of payments. The most straightforward to evaluate is a perpetual annual payment–such as rental payments. The question is what amount of money would have to be invested today in order to pay this amount in perpetuity. This involves calculating the annual income from an investment as follows:

$$A = S_0 \times i$$

Where,
A   = the annual payment

Solving the equation for the amount of capital required to fund this series of payments yields the following:

$$S_0 = \frac{A}{i}$$

Thus, to be able to make payments of $1,000 per year based on an investment at 6%, an investor would need to place $1,000 ÷ (.06) = $16,667 in the bank. This assumes that the money is placed in the bank at the beginning of the year and all annual payments take place at the end of the year.

The formula for making a series of equal payments for a fixed number of years, while fully depleting the original investment, is slightly more complicated:

$$S_0 = \frac{A}{i} \times \left[1 - \frac{1}{(1+i)^n}\right]$$

Where,

n = the number of payments

Again, this assumes that the original investment occurs at the beginning of the year and each annual payment occurs at the end of each year.

CHOOSING AN INTEREST RATE

Which interest rate should be used depends on the individual problem, the decision maker's financial situation, and prevailing market conditions. Essentially, where is the money going to come from? The interest rate represents the opportunity cost for using the money on the alternative under consideration. If the investment would involve borrowing money from the bank, then the appropriate interest rate would be the rate charged on the best loan the decision maker could obtain. If the money would be taken out of savings, then the appropriate interest rate is the prevailing rate on the decision maker's current investments or at least those that would be liquidated to finance the new investment.

For larger businesses, government agencies, and individuals with complicated investments, funds can come from numerous sources including other investments, loans, selling stock, and selling bonds. In these situations, organizations typically determine the interest rate as an average across all of the sources of funding.

The problem of choosing an interest rate and calculating the NPV of a payment can be further complicated by changing financial markets, inflation, and tax considerations.

☐ EXERCISES

1. Determine the FV for the following payments:
    a. $2,500 placed in an account for 1 year at 8% interest
    b. $5,000 placed in an account for 1 year at 4% interest
    c. $2,500 placed in an account for 2 years at 8% interest
    d. $2,500 placed in an account for 10 years at 8% interest
    e. $65,000 placed in an account for 5 years at 7% interest
    f. $2,000 placed in an account for 30 years at 7% interest

2. Determine the NPV for the following payments:
    a. A $500 payment next year, assuming 4% interest
    b. A $4,500 payment in 2 years, assuming 9% interest
    c. A $4,500 payment in 5 years, assuming 9% interest
    d. A $10,000 payment in 30 years, assuming 7% interest
    e. A $20,000 payment in 8 years, assuming 12% interest
    f. A $5,000 payment in 9 years, assuming 4% interest

3. Create a graph showing how the NPV of $10,000 changes for various values ranging from 1 to 20 years. Use an interest rate of 8%. Describe what the graph shows.

4. Create a graph showing how the NPV of a $10,000 payment five years from now changes for various interest rates ranging from 3% up to 15%. Describe what the graph shows.

5. Determine the NPV for the following multiple payments:
    a. $500 a year, forever, assuming 4% interest
    b. $120,000 a year, forever, assuming 9% interest
    c. $3,500 a year, for 4 years, assuming 8% interest
    d. $2,000 a year, for 15 years, assuming 6% interest
    e. $62,000 a year, for 3 years, assuming 11% interest
    f. $850 a year, for 2 years, assuming 7% interest

6. Create a graph showing how the NPV of a series of $10,000 payments changes for various numbers of payments ranging from 1 to 20. Use an interest rate of 8%. Describe what the graph shows.

Appendix E
OUTLINE FOR A DECISION RECOMMENDATION

An excellent decision recommendation should incorporate all of the analyses suggested in the "For Your Project" sections at the end of each chapter. This appendix indicates what might be included in each section of a final report. The section headings should correspond to the steps of the rational model, particularly from problem statement through selection, in order to highlight the reasoning behind the decision recommended.

Executive Summary

- People who read a recommendation are going to try to concisely summarize the analysis. The chances that they will get it right are greatly enhanced if they are provided with a short summary carefully prepared by the report's author. This summary should describe the problem, identify the recommended solution, and indicate the basis for the recommendation (what factors from the analysis contributed most strongly to selecting the recommended alternative). Most importantly, the executive summary should be much shorter than the report, perhaps only one page.

Problem Statement

- Describe the nature and scope of the problem studied.

- Describe the history of the problem including its cause(s) and the result of any previous attempts to solve this or similar problems.

- If the problem's structure has been represented by an influence diagram, it should be introduced here. The details of the diagram should be described in subsequent sections.

Objectives Statement

- If the problem affects more than one stakeholder, describe each of them and the basis for their concerns.

- Describe each objective.

- Be sure to identify the amount of money that might be involved and where it would come from.

- For problems that involve only one objective (typically money), the discussion of the objective might be incorporated into the problem section.

Alternatives

- If appropriate, describe how the list of alternatives considered is varied and comprehensive.

- Describe each alternative.

- If this section is particularly short, it might be combined with the forecast section.

Forecast

- Describe the basis of the forecaster's expertise, and the extent to which and in what way the forecasts could be biased.

- Describe how the forecasts were derived.

- Describe what might happen were each alternative implemented.

- Discuss the various uncertain events and the probabilities of their occurrence.

- Discuss the reliability of the forecasts. Identify confidence intervals for each parameter forecasted.

Comparison

- For problems with only one objective:

    - Identify the alternative with the best score and consider combining the comparison and selection sections.

- For problems with multiple objectives:

    - Describe the utility scales used for each non-monetary objective, and explain why each is appropriate. This typically involves discussing the procedure used to elicit them and the rationales provided by the decision maker.

    - Present a summary scorecard, if one is available and appropriate for the problem.

    - Describe the tradeoff weights, if used, and why they are appropriate.

Selection

- Describe which alternative the decision model identified as "best," and why. Describe any alternatives that scored almost as well.

- Describe any sensitivity analyses performed.

- Explain why the report includes enough information to make a good decision at this time. Alternatively, describe what additional information would be useful and how it might be obtained. Present the results of any expected value of perfect (or imperfect) information calculations.

- Describe the alternative(s) recommended and why.

Implement, Monitor, Evaluate

- A thorough recommendation should include an implementation plan that covers who will implement the plan and how, what resources are needed to execute the plan, how the solution will be presented in order to obtain acceptance by individuals who will be instrumental in its execution (what incentives will they receive), how the process of implementing the plan will be monitored, how the course of action will be evaluated (and when and by whom), and how the plan might be subsequently revised. A comprehensive description of the myriad concerns associated with these administrative steps is beyond the scope of this book.

INDEX